Neil Fawcett was called to the Bar of England and Wales in 2006 and was appointed a Deputy District Judge in 2015 sitting in the civil jurisdiction. He currently practices at the Bar from 3 Paper Buildings in the fields of Commercial and Chancery Litigation, with a particular focus on Insurance, Property, and Commercial litigation.

A Practical Guide to Business Interruption Insurance

A Practical Guide to Business Interruption Insurance

Neil Fawcett

Law Brief Publishing

Published 2022 by Law Brief Publishing, an imprint of Law Brief Publishing Ltd
30 The Parks
Minehead
Somerset
TA24 8BT

www.lawbriefpublishing.com

Paperback: 978-1-913715-77-9

PREFACE

This is a book about Business Interruption Insurance litigation. It is intended to be practical, rather than academic and focused, rather than comprehensive. When I was asked to write it in early 2021, the Supreme Court had recently handed down its judgment in the Financial Conduct Authority Test Case litigation and my colleagues in chambers and I, as well as our instructing solicitors, had been working relentlessly on around a thousand cases across a variety of industries, in a country changed almost beyond recognition by the events of the last five years.

Firms of solicitors dealing with general work have found themselves inundated with enquiries from businesses in what in normal times would be regarded as a specialised field of law, and whilst legal practice, like other fields, has adjusted in so many ways and even trials by Zoom are now commonplace, it remains to be seen how much the law itself has changed in response to the unique and quickly-changing circumstances of the pandemic.

The FCA Test Case brought clarity to some of the most common policy wordings and the Supreme Court's decision marked a departure from the "but for" test in these cases. A number of notable cases, too, clarified the law: *TKC v Allianz Insurance PLC*[1] on the construction of terms relating to loss of property and events to property, *Rockliffe Hall Ltd. v Travelers Insurance Company Ltd.*[2] on the scope of clauses incorporating lists of diseases and *Bank of New York Mellon (International) Ltd and v Cine-UK Ltd and others*[3] on commercial rent claims.

Of great practical significance to BII claims was the controversial decision in *Zuberi v Lexlaw Limited*[4]– the first time a case on Damages-based Agreements had gone as far as the Court of Appeal. In doing so, it

1[2020] EWHC 2710 (Comm)
2[2021] EWHC 412 (Comm)
3[2021] EWHC 1013 (QB)
4[2021] EWCA Civ 16

fundamentally changed the nature of DBAs, how they will now be drafted, and substantially increased their appeal to practitioners.

Nevertheless, the bulk of cases through the High Court and County Court are yet to come and the FCA has acknowledged that many claims have yet to be decided on their own myriad variations on standard wordings. The future is more uncertain than usual and I hope this guide is of some use.

The law stated in this book is believed to be correct as at 30 September 2021.

Neil Fawcett
September 2021

ACKNOWLEDGEMENTS

Emily, my ever-patient and understanding wife, to whom, along with my parents and family, I owe everything.

Henry and Eliza, who make it all worth the effort.

My dear friends, Alex, Amit, Jack, Bush and Alice.

David Berkley QC, David Parratt QC, Jessica Simor QC, James Parks, Mark Heath, David Fielder, Satish Jakhu, Chris Guy, Nick Sutton, Iryna O'Reilly, Craig Cooper and my publishers.

CONTENTS

CHAPTER ONE

COVID-19

The global Coronavirus pandemic started in Wuhan in the Hubei province of China some time towards the end of 2019. On 31st December 2019, cases of pneumonia of unknown cause were notified to the World Health Organization ("the WHO"), which, on 12th January 2020, announced the discovery of a novel coronavirus from samples obtained from Wuhan.

The virus was subsequently named SARS-Cov-2 by s.1 of the Coronavirus Act 2020, and the disease caused by it was given the designation COVID-19 in UK law:

> **1. Meaning of "coronavirus" and related terminology**
>
> (1) In this Act—
>
> > "coronavirus" means severe acute respiratory syndrome coronavirus 2 (SARS-CoV-2);
> >
> > "coronavirus disease" means COVID-19 (the official designation of the disease which can be caused by coronavirus).
>
> (2) A reference in this Act to infection or contamination, however expressed, is a reference to infection or contamination with coronavirus.
>
> (3) But a reference in this Act to persons infected by coronavirus, however expressed, does not (unless a contrary intention appears) include persons who have been infected but are clear of coronavirus (unless re-infected).

On 30th January 2020, after a meeting of its International Health Regulations (2005) Emergency Committee, the WHO declared the outbreak of COVID-19 a "Public Health Emergency of International

Concern". The first cases of COVID-19 in the UK were confirmed by the Chief Medical Officer for England on 31st January 2020.

On 10th February 2019 the government made the Health Protection (Coronavirus) Regulations 2020/129 pursuant to powers under the Public Health (Control of Disease) Act 1984, which provided ministers with emergency powers, for example in relation to detention and screening for COVID-19.

The first national lockdown was put into place by the Health Protection (Coronavirus, Business Closure) (England) Regulations 2020/327 which entered into force on 21st March 2020 at 2:00pm which required certain businesses across the UK to close. On 26th March 2020 at 1:00pm, the Health Protection (Coronavirus, Restrictions) (England) Regulations 2020/350 came into force introducing the first national lockdown across the UK, requiring businesses to close, and confining the population to their homes.

A large volume of legislation followed, dealing with business-closure, restrictions on movement, protections against eviction, limits on international travel, the imposition of a national tier-system, requirements for wearing masks and many other subjects.

At the time of writing, over a year on from the outbreak, the UK is emerging from its 3rd national lockdown, a number of vaccines are currently being distributed, new strains of coronavirus are raging in Brazil, India and now the USA and UK and the global death toll stands at over 4.12 million people. At least 130,000 of those people were in the UK: a number equivalent to the populations of Cambridge, or Gloucester.

On 21st July 2021, the Office of National Statistics ("the ONS") released figures suggesting that 3.6% of adults had reported suffering from the chronic effects of COVID-19 ("long COVID"), a figure comparable to the prevalence of coronary heart disease in the UK.

The economic effects of the pandemic have been severe and insolvency for many businesses is a real prospect, if not a reality. Some businesses were covered by insurance in the case of closure relating to pandemics such as this; others have discovered, sometimes to their surprise, that they are not.

CHAPTER TWO

GOVERNMENT INTERVENTION

It is not easy to follow the history of the restrictions imposed on businesses and individuals in the UK. Not only were numerous pieces of secondary legislation and amendments introduced, but the often-confusing guidance issued by the government has legal significance in some circumstances.

Statutory Restrictions

The three lockdowns in the UK took place on or around 21st March 2020, 5th November 2020 and 6th January 2021, and were brought into force by:

(a) the Health Protection (Coronavirus, Business Closure) (England) Regulations 2020/327 (in force on 21st March 2020 at 2:00pm) and the Health Protection (Coronavirus, Restrictions) (England) Regulations 2020/350 (in force on 26th March 2020 at 1:00pm);

(b) the Health Protection (Coronavirus, Restrictions) (England) (No. 4) Regulations (in force on 5th November 2020);

(c) the Health Protection (Coronavirus, Restrictions) (No. 3) and (All Tiers) (England) (Amendment) Regulations (in force on 6th January 2021).

The statutory restrictions applied in two pertinent respects. Firstly, they required all businesses of certain specified types to close. Secondly, they required people to stay at home. Both types of restriction had effects on businesses and are relevant for the purposes of BII policies.

Below is a summary of the key legislation classifying COVID-19 as a "notifiable disease" and then imposing restrictions on individuals and businesses. Other instruments dealing with issues not directly relating to the lockdown have been omitted, as are those relating to Scotland and Northern Ireland:

Public Restrictions (England)	**Commencement**
Health Protection (Coronavirus) Regulations 2020/129	10.02.2020 6:50am
Health Protection (Notification) (Amendment) Regulations 2020/237	05.03.2020 6:15 am
Health Protection (Coronavirus, Business Closure) (England) Regulations 2020/327	**21.03.2020 2:00pm**
Health Protection (Coronavirus, Restrictions) (England) Regulations 2020/350	26.03.2020 1:00pm
Health Protection (Coronavirus, Restrictions) (England) (Amendment) Regulations 2020/447	22.04.2020 11:00am
Health Protection (Coronavirus, Restrictions) (England) (Amendment) (No. 2) Regulations 2020/500	13.05.2020
Health Protection (Coronavirus, Restrictions) (England) (Amendment) (No. 3) Regulations 2020/558	01.06.2020
Health Protection (Coronavirus, Restrictions) (England) (Amendment) (No. 4) Regulations 2020/588	13.06.2020
Health Protection (Coronavirus, Restrictions) (No. 2) (England) Regulations 2020/684	04.07.2020

Health Protection (Coronavirus, Restrictions) (No. 2) (England) (Amendment) Regulations 2020/719	2(1), (2), (3): 11.07.2020, 2(4): 13.07.2020
Health Protection (Coronavirus, Restrictions) (No. 2) (England) (Amendment) (No. 2) Regulations 2020/788	25.07.2020
Health Protection (Coronavirus, Restrictions) (No. 2) (England) (Amendment) (No. 3) Regulations 2020/863	15.08.2020
Health Protection (Coronavirus, Restrictions) (No. 2) (England) (Amendment) (No. 4) Regulations 2020/986	14.09.2020
Health Protection (Coronavirus, Restrictions) (No. 2) (England) (Amendment) (No. 5) Regulations 2020/1029	24.09.2020 5:00am
Health Protection (Coronavirus, Restrictions) (England) (No. 3) Regulations 2020/750	18.07.2020 12:01
Health Protection (Coronavirus, Restrictions) (Self-Isolation) (England) Regulations 2020/1045	28.09.2020
Health Protection (Coronavirus, Restrictions) (England) (No. 4) Regulations 2020/1200	**05.11.2020**
Health Protection (Coronavirus, Restrictions) (England) (No. 4) (Amendment) Regulations 2020/1242	10.11.2020
Health Protection (Coronavirus, Restrictions) (England) (No. 4) (Amendment) (No. 2) Regulations 2020/1326	21.11.2020
Health Protection (Coronavirus, Restrictions) (All Tiers) (England) Regulations 2020/1374	02.12.2020

Health Protection (Coronavirus, Restrictions) (All Tiers) (England) (Amendment) Regulations 2020/1533	16.12.2020
Health Protection (Coronavirus, Restrictions) (All Tiers) (England) (Amendment) (No. 2) Regulations 2020/1572	19.12.2020
Health Protection (Coronavirus, Restrictions) (All Tiers and Obligations of Undertakings) (England) (Amendment) Regulations 2020/1611	20.12.2020 7:00am
Health Protection (Coronavirus, Restrictions) (All Tiers) (England) (Amendment) (No. 3) Regulations 2020/1646	26.12.2020
Health Protection (Coronavirus, Restrictions) (All Tiers) (England) (Amendment) (No. 4) Regulations 2020/1654	31.12.2020
Health Protection (Coronavirus, Restrictions) (No. 3) and (All Tiers) (England) (Amendment) Regulations 2021/8	**06.01.2021**
Health Protection (Coronavirus, Restrictions) (All Tiers) (England) (Amendment) Regulations 2021/53	20.01.2021
Health Protection (Coronavirus, Restrictions) (All Tiers and Self-Isolation) (England) (Amendment) Regulations 2021/97	29.01.2021 5:00pm
Health Protection (Coronavirus, Restrictions) (Steps) (England) Regulations 2021/364	29.03.2021
Health Protection (Coronavirus, Restrictions) (Steps and Local Authority Enforcement Powers) (England) (Amendment) Regulations 2021/455	12.04.2021

The 21st March 2020 Regulations

The 21st March 2020 Regulations (effective until 25th March 2020) provided:

> **2.— Requirement to close premises and businesses during the emergency**
>
> (1) A person who is responsible for carrying on a business which is listed in Part 1 of the Schedule must—
>
> (a) during the relevant period—
>
> (i) close any premises, or part of the premises, in which food or drink are sold for consumption on those premises, and
>
> (ii) cease selling food or drink for consumption on its premises; or
>
> (b) if the business sells food or drink for consumption off the premises, cease selling food or drink for consumption on its premises during the relevant period.
>
> (2) For the purposes of paragraph (1)(a), food or drink sold by a hotel or other accommodation as part of room service is not to be treated as being sold for consumption on its premises.
>
> (3) For the purposes of paragraph (1)(a)(ii) and (b), an area adjacent to the premises of the business where seating is made available for customers of the business (whether or not by the business) to be treated as part of the premises of that business.
>
> (4) A person responsible for carrying on a business which is listed in Part 2 of the Schedule must cease to carry on that business during the relevant period.

> (5) If a business listed in the Schedule ("business A") forms part of a larger business ("business B"), the person responsible for carrying on business B complies with the requirement in paragraph (1) if it closes down business A.
>
> . . .

Schedule 1 to the 21st March 2020 regulations set out lists of types of businesses that were required to close under regulation 2: restaurants, cafés, pubs, cinemas, theatres, nightclubs, spas, betting shops, and others.

The 26th March 2020 Regulations

In force from 1:00pm on 26th March 2020, until 21st April 2020, the Health Protection (Coronavirus, Restrictions) (England) Regulations 2020, repealed and replaced the 21st March 2020 Regulations and added an additional layer of restrictions, requiring the public to remain at home.

Regulations 6 and 7 set out some of the most severe intrusions into the lives of private citizens in peacetime:

> **6.— Restrictions on movement**
>
> (1) During the emergency period, no person may leave the place where they are living without reasonable excuse.
>
> (2) For the purposes of paragraph (1), a reasonable excuse includes the need—
>
> > (a) to obtain basic necessities, including food and medical supplies for those in the same household (including any pets or animals in the household) or for vulnerable persons and supplies for the essential upkeep, maintenance and functioning of the household, or the household of a vulnerable person, or to obtain money, including from any business listed in Part 3 of Schedule 2;

(b) to take exercise either alone or with other members of their household;

...

7. Restrictions on gatherings

During the emergency period, no person may participate in a gathering in a public place of more than two people except—

(a) where all the persons in the gathering are members of the same household,

(b) where the gathering is essential for work purposes,

(c) to attend a funeral,

(d) where reasonably necessary—

(i) to facilitate a house move,

(ii) to provide care or assistance to a vulnerable person, including relevant personal care within the meaning of paragraph 7(3B) of Schedule 4 to the Safeguarding of Vulnerable Groups Act 2006,

(iii) to provide emergency assistance, or

(iv) to participate in legal proceedings or fulfil a legal obligation. ...

Guidance

Identifying the specific cause of business interruption is an important aspect of pursuing a claim. That itself adds a layer of complexity at the outset of any claim because disagreements arise between insurers and businesses as to whether and to what extent a business has shut down and whether it was *required* to shut down. To that extent, the guidance issued by the government is of legal relevance.

The first public statement made by the Prime Minister, Boris Johnson, regarding restrictions was in the form of a speech on 16th March 2020, which asked the members of the public to:

1. self-isolate for 14 days if they or anyone in their household had a high temperature or a new and continuous cough;

2. to stop all non-essential contact with others and to stop all unnecessary travel; to work from home; to avoid pubs, clubs theatres and social venues; and

3. in time, isolate those with serious health conditions from social contact for 12 weeks.

On 18th March 2021, the Prime Minister gave another speech saying, amongst other things:

> "So I can announce today and Gavin Williamson making statement now in House of Commons that after schools shut their gates from Friday afternoon, they will remain closed for most pupils – for the vast majority of pupils-until further notice. I will explain what I mean by the vast majority of pupils."

On 20th March 2020, the Prime Minister gave another speech instructing "Category 1" and "Category 2" businesses[1] to close:

> "...We are collectively telling, telling cafes, pubs, bars, restaurants to close tonight as soon as they reasonably can,

1 See below, and paragraph 36 of the decision in *The Financial Conduct Authority v Arch Insurance (UK) Ltd. and Ors* [2021] UKSC 1, where the parties adopted seven categories of business for the purposes of the proceedings.

> and not to open tomorrow. Though to be clear, they can continue to provide take-out services. We're also telling nightclubs, theatres, cinemas, gyms and leisure centres to close on the same timescale...."

"Category 6" businesses were instructed by the Prime Minister, on 24th March 2020, to close.

The significance of the above guidance is that an argument developed between the FCA and insurers, described as "*the force of law point*", as to what actually necessitated closure of businesses. Although statutory restrictions came into force on 21st March 2021, some businesses closed earlier in response to the Prime Minister's guidance, which did not have the force of law. It was therefore of importance, for the construction of some policies, for the court to decide whether businesses had or had not suffered from interference where their closure was based on seemingly voluntary guidance issued before regulations came into force. As discussed later in more detail, the above guidance was categorised into "general measures" and "specific measures" for the purposes of that argument.

CHAPTER THREE

CATEGORIES OF BUSINESS

The Supreme Court in FCA 2 divided business into seven categories to assist with identification as to which types of business were required to close by the initial guidance and first tranche of statutory intervention. They are summarised as follows:

<table>
<tr>
<td>Category 1</td>
<td>1. Restaurants, including restaurants and dining rooms in hotels or members' clubs.

2.—

(1) Cafes, including workplace canteens (subject to sub-paragraph (2)), but not including—

(a) cafes or canteens at a hospital, care home or school;

(b) canteens at a prison or an establishment intended for use for naval, military or air force purposes or for the purposes of the Department of the Secretary of State responsible for defence;

(c) services providing food or drink to the homeless.

(2) Workplace canteens may remain open where there is no practical alternative for staff at that workplace to obtain food.

3. Bars, including bars in hotels or members' clubs.

4. Public houses.

Notes:

(See Health Protection (Coronavirus, Restrictions) (England) Regulations 2020/350, Sch. 2, Part 1. 26th March 2020 to 3rd July 2020)

These businesses were required to close, or cease selling any food or drink for consumption on the premises, by reg. 2(1) of the 21st March Regulations and reg. 4(1) of the 26th March Regulations.</td>
</tr>
</table>

Category 2	5. Cinemas. 6. Theatres. 7. Nightclubs. 8. Bingo halls. 9. Concert halls. 10. Museums and galleries. 11. Casinos. 12. Betting shops. 13. Spas. 14. Nail, beauty, hair salons and barbers. 15. Massage parlours. 16. Tattoo and piercing parlours. 17. Skating rinks. 18. Indoor fitness studios, gyms, swimming pools, bowling alleys, amusement arcades or soft play areas or other indoor leisure centres or facilities. 19. Funfairs (whether outdoors or indoors). 20. Playgrounds, sports courts and outdoor gyms. 21. Outdoor markets (except for stalls selling food). 22. Car showrooms. 23. Auction Houses. **Notes:** *(See Health Protection (Coronavirus, Restrictions) (England) Regulations 2020/350, Sch. 2, Part 2. 26th March 2020 to 21st April 2020).* *This list was amended a number of times subsequently.* These businesses were required to close by regulation 4(4) of the 26th March Regulations (and some had already been required to close by regulation 2(4) of the 21st March Regulations).

Category 3	24. Food retailers, including food markets, supermarkets, convenience stores and corner shops. 25. Off licences and licensed shops selling alcohol (including breweries). 26. Pharmacies (including non-dispensing pharmacies) and chemists. 27. Newsagents. 28. Homeware, building supplies and hardware stores. 29. Petrol stations. 30. Car repair and MOT services. 31. Bicycle shops. 32. Taxi or vehicle hire businesses. 33. Banks, building societies, credit unions, short term loan providers and cash points. 34. Post offices. 35. Funeral directors. 36. Laundrettes and dry cleaners. 37. Dental services, opticians, audiology services, chiropody, chiropractors, osteopaths and other medical or health services, including services relating to mental health. 38. Veterinary surgeons and pet shops. 39. Agricultural supplies shop. 40. Storage and distribution facilities, including delivery drop off or collection points, where the facilities are in the premises of a business included in this Part. 41. Car parks. 42. Public toilets. **Notes:** *(See Health Protection (Coronavirus, Restrictions) (England) Regulations 2020/350, Sch. 2, Part 3. 26th March 2020 to 21st April 2020).* *This list was amended a number of times subsequently.* These businesses were allowed to remain open, and excluded from the scope of reg. 5(1) of the 26th March Regulations.

Category 4	Businesses (excluding Category 3 businesses) offering goods for sale or for hire in a shop, or library services, which were required by reg. 5(1) not to admit any customers or users to their premises.
Category 5	Businesses not mentioned in the 21st March Regulations or the 26th March Regulations at all, including professional service firms such as accountants and lawyers, as well as construction and manufacturing businesses.
Category 6	Businesses providing holiday accommodation, which were affected by reg. 5(3) of the 26th March Regulations.
Category 7	Places of worship, which were affected by reg. 5(5) of the 26th March Regulations, together with nurseries and schools.

CHAPTER FOUR

THE FCA TEST CASE

Shortly after the events of March 2020, on 9th June 2020, the Financial Conduct Authority ("the FCA") brought proceedings in the High Court as the financial regulator under the framework then provided under Practice Direction 51M (now paragraphs 6.1 to 6.5 of PD 63AA) of the Civil Procedure Rules 1998.

The practice direction provides for a Financial Market Test Case Scheme to allow interested parties to bring a claim, by mutual agreement, for determination in the Financial List without having to show a cause of action between them.

The criterion under paragraph 6.1 of a claim being a "qualifying claim" is met if the claim "*raises issues of general importance in relation to which immediately relevant authoritative English law guidance is needed*". In those circumstances, the claim can be determined *without* there needing to be a cause of action between the parties to the proceedings. Under paragraph 6.3, any person "*who is or was actively in business in the relevant market*" may bring proceedings against any other person "*who is or was actively in business in the relevant market*", if:

(a) proceedings are issued by mutual agreement; and

(b) the parties have opposing interests as to how the issues under the law of England and Wales should be resolved.

The FCA, the main insurers and interveners including the Hiscox Action Group sought declarations from the High Court on general principles to be applied in BII cases. The court, comprising Flaux LJ and Butcher J, handed down judgment on 15th September 2020 in *The Financial Conduct Authority v Arch Insurance (UK) Ltd. and Ors* [2020] EWHC 2448 (Comm) (now referred to herein as "FCA 1").

The decision was appealed, bypassing the Court of Appeal, directly to the Supreme Court which handed down judgment on 15th January 2021 in *The Financial Conduct Authority v Arch Insurance (UK) Ltd. and Ors* [2021] UKSC 1 (now referred to herein as "FCA 2").

CHAPTER FIVE

POLICIES AND CLAUSES

The Policy

Business Interruption Insurance ("BII") policies are contractual in nature, and the usual rules of contractual interpretation apply to them but there is nevertheless a substantial body of case-law specific to the subject.

The main contractual documents comprise the policy schedule and the policy wording. Ordinarily, both make reference to each other and are read together as a contractual instrument. It is quite common to find that insurance schedules set out the details specific to the individual business, such as the policy limit, the indemnity period, the optional extras and sometimes specific applicable clauses. Policy wordings are more usually in standard forms published by the main insurers online.

Typically, BII forms one part of the insurance within a policy. Many insurers provide a "Commercial Combined" policy wording or wordings specific to certain industries, such as pubs, restaurants, children's nurseries, hotels, or manufacturers, for example, each with clauses relevant to that industry. Within policies there will often be clauses providing cover for fire, theft, destruction of property, or (often) pay-outs for key staff who leave when they win the lottery.

Most policies break their BII sections down into subsections dealing with the basic cover for interruption to business, and subsections dealing with extensions to that cover. The basic cover is normally specified to arise solely as a result of physical property damage in a number of defined circumstances. The extensions to cover are ordinarily those circumstances in which the insurer agrees to pay out for interruption to business caused by things other than physical property damage, like devastating global pandemics.

Other Documents

Although most policies comprise a schedule and a policy wording, It is important to check whether additional documents may have been incorporated into the contract of insurance. Sometimes other documents are attached to the policy, or reference is made to them by words which have the effect of incorporating them, rather than just reciting them, as in *Wheelton v Hardisty*, where a policy proposal was incorporated on the basis of words which indicated that the contract was framed on the proposal[2].

In addition to documents which are incorporated, parties may also admit in evidence pre-contractual documents for the purpose of ascertaining the objective intentions of the parties in cases of ambiguity. See, for example, *Hordern v Commercial Union Insurance Co*[3]:

> "If the question had been one of the construction of the policy alone, it would be for the Court; but when once the evidence disclosed that on that policy there was a latent ambiguity, and that it was necessary to go into the consideration of other documents, and to resort to parol evidence to solve that ambiguity, their Lordships consider that there it ceased to be a question merely of construction of the instrument, and raised a question of fact to be determined by the jury, that question being, as already pointed out, whether the policy covered the goods, that is to say, whether it covered that portion of the premises in which these goods actually were stored at the time of the fire".

2 *Wheelton v Hardisty* (1857) 8 E. & B. 232. at 95.

3 (1887) 56 L.J.P.C. 78.

The Insurer

In practice, it is often obvious who the insurer is, especially when the insurer is a large, well-known and singular entity, like Allianz Plc. Confusion sometimes arises, however, when the insurer is described in the policy documents in a number of less specific ways.

How Insurers are Defined

Policies vary widely in how they specify the identity of the insurer and there is no standard method of doing so. Sometimes policy schedules include the name of the insurer on the front page or specify different insurers for different sections of the insurance policy. Many policies contain a list of definitions towards the beginning of the policy wording. In that list "the Insurer", "We/Us", "the Company" and other variations appear, to describe the identity of the insurer.

Lloyd's Syndicates

Many policies are underwritten by Lloyd's syndicates and the definition of "Insurer" in the policy may simply provide "Certain Lloyd's Underwriters", or "Syndicate 1234 at Lloyd's". Lloyd's of London itself is a corporate society, incorporated under the Lloyd's Act 1871, which operates an insurance and reinsurance market in London and is under statutory control in the form of the Lloyd's Acts 1871 to 1982 and the Financial Services and Markets Act 2000. Lloyd's is not an underwriter with liability to the insured, but rather a society which runs the Lloyd's insurance market: a collection of individual and corporate underwriters, known as "Names", or "Members" who group themselves into syndicates[4] and subscribe to a particular insurance policy taking on liability to the insured.

---

4 An updated list of all currently operating Lloyd's syndicates is maintained in tabular form at https://ldc.lloyds.com/market-directory

A Lloyd's syndicate is not a legal entity or a partnership, but a group of Names who have joined a particular syndicate for a particular underwriting year. Each policy issued at Lloyd's consists of individual contracts made on behalf of individual Names[5], with each Name being liable to the insured only *for his own share* of the insurance provided under a policy[6] (i.e. the liability is not *joint and* several).

Underwriting Agents

Section 8(2) of the Lloyd's Act 1982, helps to explain the purpose of underwriting agents:

> **8.— Insurance business**
>
> ...
>
> (2) An underwriting member (not being himself an underwriting agent) shall underwrite contracts of insurance at Lloyd's only through an underwriting agent.
>
> ...

Underwriting agents not only manage syndicates, winding them down, adding or removing Names, but also advise Names on which syndicates to join, on their allocation of premiums, on the nature of the risk they take on or in practice act in a role combining both advice and management.

Policies frequently make reference to underwriting agents, giving their contact detail within the policy definitions or within the section sometimes entitled "How to Claim". Such underwriting agents ought not to be confused with brokers, who act not only for the insured, but also on behalf of underwriting agents. Underwriting agents do not

---

5 See *Society of Lloyd's v Robinson* [1999] 1 W.L.R. 756 at 760.

6 Lloyd's Act 1982, s.8(1).

themselves take on liability to insureds, despite words apt to confuse which state "*This insurance is provided by X Agents on behalf of Y*".

The Room and the Slip

Insurance at Lloyd's is placed by "Lloyd's brokers"[7], who have access to "The Room", which means "*the principle room or rooms in the Society's premises in the city of London for the time being designated by the Council for the purposes of underwriting*"[8]. A broker will write down the cover required using abbreviations on a slip and take the slip round underwriters in the Room, who, if they agree to provide cover, will initial a line on the slip confirming their agreement and the percentage of the insurance they agree to underwrite. The broker will continue until 100 per cent of the insurance is subscribed and deposit the slip at the Lloyd's Policy Signing Office ("LPSO"), which will execute an insurance policy which it certifies is in conformity with the insurance abbreviated on the slip, in the name of the various underwriters[9].

Crucially, there is a binding contract of insurance as soon as a particular underwriter has initialled the slip, and the final policy is executed by the LPSO with the authority of the underwriters, evidence by their initials on the slip, as if the underwriters themselves had executed the engrossed policy[10].

The Correct Defendant in a Claim

The position as to legal liability and privity of contract is as explained above. The convention, however, is that a claim for an indemnity by Joe Bloggs against his insurers would be brought for ease in the form

---

7 Per Lloyd's Act 1982, s.2(1): "Lloyd's broker" means a partnership or body corporate permitted by the Council to describe itself as a Lloyd's broker".

8 Ibid.

9 Eagle Star Insurance Co Ltd v Spratt [1971] 2 Lloyd's Rep. 116

10 General Reinsurance Corporation and Others v Forsakringsaktiebolaget Fennia Patria [1983] Q.B. 856.

"*Joe Bloggs v Certain Underwriters at Lloyd's*". The various underwriters in the relevant syndicate are usually then included in a schedule of defendants on the claim form, as follows:

Claimant(s) name(s) and address(es) including postcode:

Joe Bloggs, 123 Cabbage Road, Walsall WS1 123.

Defendant(s) name and address(es) including postcode:

Certain Underwriters at Lloyd's subscribing to Policy Number CCOM/1234A,[below]/[as in Schedule of Defendants]:

1. TVA 1991 c/o Wales and Worcester Bathurst Ltd., Insurance House, London E1 123

2. SYNJON c/o David Johnson Syndicates Ltd., 5 Bank House, London E1 345

3. JA 2000 c/o Joanne Evans, 15 Gold Apartments, London SW1X 123

The RSA Example

An example[11] of the basic BII cover ("RSA 3") provided by Royal and Sun Alliance Plc is:

"Cover

In the event of ***Business Interruption We*** *will pay to* ***You*** *in respect of each item in the* ***Schedule*** *the amount of loss resulting from such interruption or interference provided that at the time of the happening of the loss destruction or* ***Damage*** *there is an insurance in force covering* ***Your*** *interest in the*

11 Categorised as "RSA 3" in FCA 1. Square brackets contain the references used in that case.

> ***Property** at the **Premises** against such loss destruction or **Damage** and that:*
>
> *a) payment shall have been made or liability admitted therefore [sic]; or*
>
> *b) payment would have been made or liability admitted [sic] but for the operation of a proviso in such insurance excluding liability for losses below a specified amount."*

RSA 3 provides a number of extensions to that basic property-damage cover:

i. *"Interruption or interference with "the **Business**" in consequence of "an **Incident**" at any site not in the occupation of the insured, within the territorial limits of the policy, at which the insured is carrying out a contract [Extension iii, "Contract Sites"];*

ii. *Interruption or interference with "the **Business**" carried on at "the **Premises**" following loss of an employee as a result of the death or injury to the employee or the employee winning a lottery or similar prize in an amount exceeding £100,000 [Extension v, "Essential Employees"];*

iii. *Interruption or interference with "the **Business**" "as a result of the accidental failure of supply of" electricity, gas, water or telecommunications services at "the **Premises**" [Extension vi, "Failure of Supply"];*

iv. *Interruption or interference with "the **Business**" as a result of loss, destruction or damage to property in the "**Vicinity**" of "the **Premises**" which prevents or hinders the use of or access to "the **Premises**" or leads to a loss of attraction to the "**Business**", or of the actions of a competent Public Authority due to an emergency likely to endanger life or property in the "Vicinity" of "the **Premises**" [Extensions ix, x and xi, "Prevention of Access"];*

v. *Interruption or interference with "the **Business**" as a result of loss, destruction or damage to property at, broadly, the facilities or premises of public utilities [Extension xii, "Public Utilities"], or of specified customers [Extension xiii, "Specified Customers"], or of specified suppliers [Extension xiv, "Specified Suppliers"], or at sites where the insured's goods are stored [Extension xv, "Storage Sites"];*

vi. *Interruption or interference with "the **Business**" as a result of loss, destruction or damage to the insured's property whilst in transit in Great Britain or Northern Ireland [Extension xvi, "Transit"]."*

In the context of the pandemic, the most relevant extension is Extension vii "Infectious Diseases":

> *"**We** shall indemnify You in respect of interruption or interference with the **Business** during the **Indemnity Period** following:*
>
> *a) any*
>
> > *i. occurrence of a Notifiable Disease (as defined below) at the **Premises** or attributable to food or drink supplied from the **Premises;***
> >
> > *ii. discovery of an organism at the **Premises** likely to result in the occurrence of a Notifiable Disease;*
> >
> > *iii. occurrence of a Notifiable Disease within a radius of 25 miles of the **Premises;***
>
> *b) the discovery of vermin or pests at the Premises which causes restrictions on the use of the **Premises** on the order or advice of the competent local authority;*
>
> *c) any accident causing defects in the drains or other sanitary arrangements at the Premises which causes restrictions on the*

*use of the **Premises** on the order or advice of the competent local authority; or*

*d) any occurrence of murder or suicide at the **Premises**.*

Additional Definition in respect of Notifiable Diseases

1. Notifiable Disease shall mean illness sustained by any person resulting from:

i. food or drink poisoning; or

ii. any human infectious or human contagious disease excluding Acquired Immune Deficiency Syndrome (AIDS) or an AIDS related condition an outbreak of which the competent local authority has stipulated shall be notified to them

2. For the purposes of this clause:

***Indemnity Period** shall mean the period during which the results of the **Business** shall be affected in consequence of the occurrence discovery or accident beginning:*

i. in the case of a) and d) above with the date of the occurrence or discovery; or

*ii. in the case of b) and c) above the date from which the restrictions on the **Premises** applied; and ending not later than the Maximum **Indemnity Period** thereafter shown below.*

***Premises** shall mean only those locations stated in the **Premises** definition. In the event that the section includes an extension which deems loss destruction or **Damage** at other locations to be an **Incident** such extension shall not apply to this clause.*

3. We shall not be liable under this clause for any costs incurred in the cleaning repair replacement recall or checking of Property

*4. We shall only be liable for the loss arising at those **Premises** which are directly affected by the occurrence discovery or accident Maximum **Indemnity Period** shall mean 3 months"*

Most policies provide variations on the above example but it is normally difficult to define more than general principles because policies, like any contract, will always be interpreted based on the contracting parties' reasonably ascertainable intentions at the time the contract was entered into. The wording of the above clause and similar clauses forms the basis for much of the argument between businesses and insurers in the context of the COVID-19 pandemic.

What arises frequently in discussion of the various types of clauses, however, is reference to "disease clauses", "denial of access clauses" and "hybrid clauses". These were summarised helpfully in FCA 2 (see para. 4) as follows:

Disease clauses	Clauses which, in general, provide cover for business interruption losses resulting from the occurrence of a notifiable disease, such as COVID-19, at or within a specified distance of the business premises.
Prevention/denial of access clauses	Clauses which, in general, provide cover for business interruption losses resulting from public authority intervention preventing or hindering access to, or use of, the business premises, without particular reference to the occurrence of disease.
Hybrid clauses	Clauses which combine the main elements of the disease and prevention of access clauses. In general terms, such hybrid clauses might provide cover for closure by a public authority "as a result of an occurrence of a notifiable disease" within the policy area.

CHAPTER SIX

THE NATURE OF INSURANCE POLICIES

General Principles

Insurance policies are contracts and, in general terms, the usual principles of contractual interpretation apply to them. There are numerous examples of courts taking that approach[12].

It therefore follows that the court will seek to ascertain the objective intentions of the contracting parties at the time the contract was concluded. As usual, that is to be contrasted with the actual, or subjective, intentions of the parties to the insurance contract. That is of particular relevance in business interruption cases because the insurance often provides cover for perils which include lists of diseases, the meaning of which it would be difficult to ascertain with reference to what the parties were actually, or subjectively, thinking at the time of the placement of the insurance.

A useful summary of the general principles of interpretation was given in *Arnold v Britton,* by Lord Neuberger[13]:

(a) reliance placed in some cases on commercial common sense and surrounding circumstances was not to be invoked to

12 *Hart v Standard Marine Insurance Co* (1889) 22 Q.B.D. 499, or, for an overview of the cases stating that principle, see *Sanday & Co. v British and Foreign Marine Insurance Company.* [1915] 2 K.B. 781, per Swinfen Eady LJ at 813 and *Sirius International Insurance Co (Publ) v FAI General Insurance Ltd* [2004] UKHL 54, [2004] 1 W.L.R. 3251 at [18]–[19].

13 [2015] UKSC 36; [2015] A.C. 1619.

undervalue the importance of the language of the provision which is to be construed;

(b) the less clear the words used were, the more ready the court could properly be to depart from their natural meaning, but that did not justify departing from the natural meaning;

(c) commercial common sense was not to be invoked retrospectively, so that the mere fact that a contractual arrangement has worked out badly, or even disastrously, for one of the parties was not a reason for departing from the natural language;

(d) a court should be very slow to reject the natural meaning of a provision as correct simply because it appeared to be a very imprudent term for one of the parties to have agreed;

(e) when interpreting a contractual provision, the court could only take into account facts or circumstances which existed at the time that the contract was made, and which were known or reasonably available to both parties; and

(f) if an event subsequently occurred which was plainly not intended or contemplated by the parties, if it was clear what the parties would have intended, the court would give effect to that intention.

The Court in FCA 1 quoted *Wood v Capita Insurance Services Ltd*[14] as a summary of the principles following *Arnold v Britton* and *Rainy Sky SA v Kookmin Bank*[15]:

"10. The court's task is to ascertain the objective meaning of the language which the parties have chosen to express

14 [2017] UKSC 24, [2017] AC 1173.

15 [2011] UKSC 50.

their agreement. It has long been accepted that this is not a literalist exercise focused solely on a parsing of the wording of the particular clause but that the court must consider the contract as a whole and, depending on the nature, formality and quality of drafting of the contract, give more or less weight to elements of the wider context in reaching its view as to that objective meaning. In *Prenn v Simmonds* [1971] 1 WLR 1381, 1383H- 1385D and in *Reardon Smith Line Ltd v Yngvar Hansen- Tangen (trading as HE Hansen-Tangen)* [1976] 1 WLR 989, 997, Lord Wilberforce affirmed the potential relevance to the task of interpreting the parties' contract of the factual background known to the parties at or before the date of the contract, excluding evidence of the prior negotiations. When in his celebrated judgment in *Investors Compensation Scheme Ltd v West Bromwich Building Society* [1998] 1 WLR 896, 912-913 Lord Hoffmann reformulated the principles of contractual interpretation, some saw his second principle, which allowed consideration of the whole relevant factual background available to the parties at the time of the contract, as signalling a break with the past. But Lord Bingham of Cornhill in an extrajudicial writing, "*A New Thing Under the Sun? The Interpretation of Contracts and the ICS decision*" (2008) 12 Edin LR 374, persuasively demonstrated that the idea of the court putting itself in the shoes of the contracting parties had a long pedigree.

11. Lord Clarke of Stone-cum-Ebony JSC elegantly summarised the approach to construction in the *Rainy Sky* case [2011] 1 WLR 2900, para 21f. In the *Arnold* case [2015] AC 1619 all of the judgments confirmed the approach in the *Rainy Sky* case: Lord Neuberger of Abbotsbury PSC, paras 13-14; Lord Hodge JSC, para 76 and Lord Carnwath JSC, para 108. Interpretation is, as Lord Clarke JSC stated in the *Rainy Sky* case (para 21), a unitary exercise; where there are rival meanings, the court can give weight to the implications of rival constructions by reaching a view as to which construction is more consistent

with business common sense. But, in striking a balance between the indications given by the language and the implications of the competing constructions the court must consider the quality of drafting of the clause (the *Rainy Sky* case, para 26, citing Mance LJ in *Gan Insurance Co Ltd v Tai Ping Insurance Co Ltd* (No 2) [2001] 2 All ER (Comm) 299, paras 13, 16); and it must also be alive to the possibility that one side may have agreed to something which with hindsight did not serve his interest: the *Arnold* case, paras 20, 77. Similarly, the court must not lose sight of the possibility that a provision may be a negotiated compromise or that the negotiators were not able to agree more precise terms.

12. This unitary exercise involves an iterative process by which each suggested interpretation is checked against the provisions of the contract and its commercial consequences are investigated: the *Arnold* case, para 77 citing In re *Sigma Finance Corpn* [2010] 1 All ER 571, para 12, per Lord Mance JSC. To my mind once one has read the language in dispute and the relevant parts of the contract that provide its context, it does not matter whether the more detailed analysis commences with the factual background and the implications of rival constructions or a close examination of the relevant language in the contract, so long as the court balances the indications given by each.

13. Textualism and contextualism are not conflicting paradigms in a battle for exclusive occupation of the field of contractual interpretation. Rather, the lawyer and the judge, when interpreting any contract, can use them as tools to ascertain the objective meaning of the language which the parties have chosen to express their agreement. The extent to which each tool will assist the court in its task will vary according to the circumstances of the particular agreement or agreements. Some agreements may be successfully interpreted principally by textual analysis, for example because of their sophistication and complexity and

because they have been negotiated and prepared with the assistance of skilled professionals. The correct interpretation of other contracts may be achieved by a greater emphasis on the factual matrix, for example because of their informality, brevity or the absence of skilled professional assistance. But negotiators of complex formal contracts may often not achieve a logical and coherent text because of, for example, the conflicting aims of the parties, failures of communication, differing drafting practices, or deadlines which require the parties to compromise in order to reach agreement. There may often therefore be provisions in a detailed professionally drawn contract which lack clarity and the lawyer or judge in interpreting such provisions may be particularly helped by considering the factual matrix and the purpose of similar provisions in contracts of the same type. The iterative process, of which Lord Mance JSC spoke in *Sigma Finance Corpn* [2010] 1 All ER 571, para 12, assists the lawyer or judge to ascertain the objective meaning of disputed provisions."

The Indemnity

In normal circumstances, the claim for a pay-out under the terms of an insurance policy is not a claim for damages for breach of contract, but a claim for payment of a contractual indemnity in circumstances defined by the contract of insurance. The significance of that cannot be overstated because it is a common misconception and has application not only as to the level of loss which may be indemnified and to the subject of double insurance but also must be distinguished from actual claims for breach of the insurance contract in the context of The Insurance Act 2015, s.13A.

The Premium

Channel J in *Prudential Insurance Co v Inland Revenue Commissioners*[16] defined insurance as "*a contract whereby for some consideration, usually but not necessarily for periodical payments called premiums, you secure to yourself some benefit, usually but not necessarily the payment of a sum of money, upon the happening of some event.*".

The premium in insurance contracts is assessed with reference to risk, and may not be reflective of the cost to the insurer of providing the policy, as for example, a solicitor's fees might be assessed with reference to the work carried out. Premiums are often provided for in specific terms in policy wordings.

Whilst there is no general rule that premiums must be paid before an insurance claim can be made, insurers may have remedies in the event of non-payment: a) to bring a claim for payment of the premium; b) to refuse to indemnify a claim; or c) to forfeit the policy. In the first instance those remedies are matters of contract.

Contra Proferentem

Introduction

In broad terms, the common-law rule of *contra proferentem*[17] means that where there is ambiguity in the terms of a contract, that ambiguity ought to be resolved in favour of the party who did not draft the wording. The party who is relying on the contract is known as "*the proferens*". The principle is most often of relevance in relation to exemption clauses, although, one has to be careful in insurance

---

16 [1904] 2 K.B. 658.

17 Fully, "verba chartarum fortius accipiuntur contra proferentem" (and more recently a principle rather than a rule).

contracts to distinguish between exemption/exclusion clauses and what are, in reality, terms which simply delineate the scope of cover.

Modern Application

Although the principle is often described as being of decreasing importance in the context of modern commercial contracts (sometimes referred to as a principle of "last resort"[18]) it is often argued in modern commercial cases, particularly in cases involving the interpretation of exemption clauses. In FCA 1, for example, although the court said at paragraph 373 "*The applicable principles are as summarised by the judge in Crowden and there is no place for the application of the principle of contra proferentem, to the extent that principle has any application in the modern law of construction of contracts.*", it expressed the view at paragraph 118 that "*while we do not consider it necessary to resort to it, this would be one of the few cases in which it would be appropriate to apply a principle of contra proferentem.*".

Although *contra proferentem* was not referred to in the *Rainy Sky* case, in *Impact Funding Solutions Limited (Respondent) v AIG Europe Insurance Ltd. (formerly known as Chartis Insurance (UK) Ltd.)*[19] (quoted in FCA 1), the Supreme Court had to consider the interpretation of an exclusion clause and, after stating the general principles of contractual construction, observed:

> "6. … As I see no ambiguity in the way that the Policy defined its cover and as the exclusion clause reflected what The Law Society of England and Wales as the regulator of the solicitors' profession had authorised as a limitation of professional indemnity cover, I see no role in this case for the doctrine of interpretation contra proferentem."

---

18 E.g., Westminster City Council v Sports and Leisure Management Limited [2021] EWHC 98 (TCC) at para. 74.

19 [2016] UKSC 57, [2017] AC 73. See also Burnett or Grant v International Insurance Co of Hanover Ltd [2021] UKSC 12 which affirmed Impact Funding Solutions Ltd.

The authors of *Chitty on Contracts*[20], citing *Tektrol Ltd v International Insurance Co of Hanover Ltd*[21], express the view that it is "*one rule of construction applicable to ordinary contracts which applies with particular force in the context of insurance contracts*".

In *Taylor v Rive Droite Music Ltd.*[22], Neuberger LJ expressed a view on the modern application of *contra proferentem*:

> 142. I know of no principle which requires one to lean in favour of a construction which would give a production company a monopoly over all the output of an artist during the period of an agreement such as this. Indeed, if there is any presumption in that connection, it seems to me that it would be in the opposite sense in a case such as the present, essentially for two reasons. First, Mr Barry's Agreement was in a standard form prepared by RDM and used by it virtually routinely; contra proferentem, while no doubt enjoying a more limited and rather weaker role than it used to have, may still sometimes be of assistance when construing a contract which is in the standard form of one of the parties. Secondly, if it would be right to approach a contract such as this with any particular bias, it seems to me that it should be one which is against monopoly, restraint of trade and impairing an artist's freedom to exploit his work commercially.

Most recently in *Triple Point Technology, Inc v PTT Public Company Ltd*[23], on the subject of exclusion clauses, the Supreme Court quoted with approval the view of Andrew Burrows QC in *Federal Republic of Nigeria v JP Morgan Chase Bank NA* [2019] EWHC 347 (Comm), at

---

20 Thirty-third Edition, at 42-077.

21 [2005] EWCA Civ 845, [2005] 1 All E.R. (Comm) 132.

22 [2006] E.M.L.R. 4.

23 [2021] UKSC 29

para 34, that *contra proferentem* had been subsumed into the wider principle that parties to contracts ought to use clear words to give up a valuable right:

> "Applying the modern approach, the force of what was the *contra proferentem* rule is embraced by recognising that a party is unlikely to have agreed to give
>
> up a valuable right that it would otherwise have had without clear words. And as Moore-Bick LJ put it in the *Stocznia* case, at para 23, 'The more valuable the right, the clearer the language will need to be'. So, for example, clear words will generally be needed before a court will conclude that the agreement excludes a party's liability for its own negligence."

The Principle of Contra Proferentem

In order for the principle to have any application, there has to be genuine ambiguity in the terms of the contract. Genuine ambiguity ought to be distinguished from language capable of reasonable interpretation, but, more than that, it may be that the language involves a degree of uncertainty which could give rise to a reasonable debate over its meaning and extent, or even be contradictory yet still be unambiguous for the purposes of the principle of *contra proferentem.* The court ought to be left in genuine doubt, after applying the ordinary principles of construction, which of two meanings is correct.

McCardie J, sitting in the High Court in *Yorke v Yorkshire Insurance Company Ltd.*[24] had to consider the meaning of a question raised of a prospective insured by the insurer prior to a life insurance policy being agreed. The insurer's question was "What illnesses have you suffered?". The answer was "None, of any consequence". The question and answer were incorporated into the terms of the policy. Upon the insured's

---

24 [1918] 1 K.B. 662.

death, the insurer declined cover because the insured had failed to disclose that he had suffered from heart trouble, insomnia and addiction to veronal (barbital). The plaintiff argued that the insurer's question was ambiguous because it permitted of varying interpretations of the word "illness", either relating to the quality or condition of being ill, or to a specific disease and ought to be construed *contra proferentem* in favour of the plaintiff.

In *Yorke*, the court took the view that the question was of the sort that often came before the courts on questions of fact. It could be said, for example, that as between a headache and "brain fever", one set of facts may amount to an "illness" and the other might not. An intermediate case might very well give rise to doubt, yet that doubt was not an ambiguity, but a matter for the court's decision, as in cases where "reasonable time" or "criminal negligence" presented a similar difficulty. A case which demonstrated the point well, and which compared favourably in the view of McCardie J, was *Hutchinson v National Loan Fund Life Assurance Society* [25], where the court had to consider the question "Are you in good health?", which might cause difficulty in giving a precise definition. Lord Fullerton described "good health" as being "*the perfect conscious enjoyment of all of one's faculties and functions, and the conscious freedom from any ailment affecting them, or any symptom of ailment*". McCardie J's view was:

> "... I venture to think that a man may be in good health although he lacks the full possession of that exultant and joyous vitality indicated by Lord Fullerton. Even a pessimist may be a fit subject of life insurance.
>
> A jury can be relied on to know the meaning of the phrase "good health" as employed in the usual affairs of life, just as they will know the meaning of the words "sober and temperate" as used by the ordinary man in the omnibus, the office, or the restaurant. A question may be a question

25 (1845) 7 D. 467, 478.

> of fact although the element of opinion is involved therein. In the present case I think that the jury were amply justified in forming the view that the illness from which Smith suffered in 1911 was an illness of consequence."

Perhaps counter-intuitively, there is a distinction to be drawn between cases of ambiguity and cases of outright contradiction. For example, in the High Court case of *Plevin v DAS Legal Expenses Insurance Company Ltd.*[26], HHJ Pearce took the view that the central problem in an insurance policy was the contradiction between the terms of the policy wording and the policy schedule, such that there was no ambiguity that should lead to the application of the *contra proferentem* principle. Instead, the court held that there was a contradiction which could be resolved on the basis that the parties' objective intentions could be inferred more accurately from the individualised terms of the schedule, rather than the generic terms of the policy wording, and the language of the schedule could be given precedence.

Although *contra proferentem* is often applied in cases where one party is dealing on the other's standard terms, as is common in insurance cases, there is no strict limitation of that sort[27].

Examples of the Application of Contra Proferentem

In *Pratt v Aigaion Insurance Co SA.*[28], the owner of a small fishing trawler claimed an indemnity from the insurer when a fire broke out on board, as a result of an electrical fault, whilst the crew were ashore. The vessel was insured subject to a condition that "*Owner and/or Owner's*

26 [2019] EWHC 1339 (Comm) at [80].

27 As an example, see *Gan Insurance Co Ltd v Tai Ping Insurance Co Ltd.* [2001] C.L.C 1103, a case of re-insurance in slip form, where an issue of construction of a claims co-operation clause in standard form "*Scor (U.K.) Clause 0124/83*'", not the standard terms of either of the parties, but required by the re-insurer, Gan, to be incorporated, and who was therefore the *proferens*.

28 [2008] EWCA Civ 1314.

experienced Skipper on board and in charge at all times and one experienced crew member.". The Court of Appeal decided that the clause should be construed *contra proferentem* because there was an ambiguity as to the extent to which the clause ought to be qualified. The ambiguity was as to whether the clause applied at all times, even when the vessel was, as was common, tied up safely with the generator running, or whether the clause applied only when the vessel was at sea.

Nobahar-Cookson & Anor v Hut Group Ltd.[29] concerned an appeal against a decision to disapply the *contra proferentem* principle when interpreting a contractual time limit for the making of warranty claims pursuant to a share purchase agreement, which read "*The Sellers will not be liable for any Claim unless the Buyer serves notice of the Claim on the Sellers (specifying in reasonable detail the nature of the Claim and, so far is practicable, the amount claimed in respect it) as soon as reasonably practicable and in any event within 20 Business Days after becoming aware of the matter.*". Briggs LJ affirmed the continued relevance of the *contra proferentem* principle in relation to exclusion clauses and was assisted by the principle in deciding what the words "aware of the matter" meant, saying:

> "38. In conclusion therefore, I consider that a purposive interpretation of clause 5.1 on a fairly narrow balance favours the judge's conclusion, but that it is significantly reinforced by being the narrower of the available interpretations of a seriously ambiguous exclusion clause. In this perhaps unusual case, a thoroughly modern recourse to purposive construction happily marches hand in hand with a perhaps more old-fashioned recourse to rules or canons of construction, which continue to assist the court where all else fails."

29 [2016] 1 C.L.C. 573.

At [116-118] in FCA 1, the court expressed its view on circumstances in which the application of *contra proferentem* would be appropriate (emphasis added):

> "116. While RSA seeks to rely on the appearance of the word "epidemic" within Exclusion L, it appears to us that this reliance carries no conviction. "Epidemic" is not alone in the list but, as we have said, is in the company of "poisoning" and "disease". As we have said, we find it impossible to consider that loss as a result of these matters insofar as expressly covered under Extension vii, was intended to be excluded by this General Exclusion. Furthermore, the list of diseases which, even at the time of the conclusion of the contracts of insurance, were required to be notified to the competent local authority included some, such as SARS, which might undoubtedly give rise to an epidemic; and furthermore Notifiable Diseases as defined in Extension vii were not a closed category, and clearly a newly occurring disease giving rise to an epidemic would be likely to lead to a requirement for notification, as indeed happened with COVID-19. Accordingly, there is cover under Extension vii for certain losses following an epidemic, and for the same reasons as apply to "poisoning" and "disease" we find it impossible to accept that the general exclusion was intended to withdraw such express cover.
>
> 117. We consider that the correct construction of the policy is that sub-clause L(b) (bis) must be understood as meaning that the terms of the exclusion were not intended to override express grants of cover, or at least was not intended to apply to the disease clauses in Extension vii. It seems likely that L(b)(bis) was included precisely to cater for the possibility that, without it, General Exclusion L might not fit well with other terms of the policy in which it was being included. L(b)(bis) is not confined to preserving the effect of other exclusions in the policy, because the first part of the clause applies to "all other terms and conditions

> of the Policy", and the second part of the clause applies to a particular class, namely exclusions, which are "especially", which connotes not exclusively, not to be superseded. It is therefore wide enough, in our view, to apply to cases such as the present, in order to avoid the absurdity, and potential unfairness, of an express grant of cover being eliminated by a General Exclusion dealing with a range of matters most of which are irrelevant to the cover involved.
>
> 118. Finally, under this heading we should say, while we do not consider it necessary to resort to it, <u>this would be one of the few cases in which it would be appropriate to apply a principle of contra proferentem</u>."

<u>Ejusdem generis</u>

Contractual terms have to be interpreted in context[30]. The principle of *ejusdem generis*[31] is little more than an application of that principle. As said by Lewison LJ in *The Interpretation of Contracts* 7th Edn. at 7.130, using the formulation of Vaughan Williams LJ in *Lambourn v McLellan*[32]:

> "If it is found that things described by particular words have some common characteristic which constitutes them a genus, the general words which follow them ought to be limited to things of that genus."

---

30 Per Lord Collins in *Re Sigma Finance Corp (In Administration)* [2009] UKSC 2: "An over-literal interpretation of one provision without regard to the whole may distort or lustrate the commercial purpose. This is one of those too frequent cases where a document has been subjected to the type of textual analysis more appropriate to the Interpretation of tax legislation which has been the subject of detailed scrutiny at all committee stages than to an instrument securing commercial obligations.".

31 Literally, "of the same kind".

32 [1903] 2 Ch. 268.

The principle is often of relevance in the construction of lists within contracts which follow the pattern "X, Y and others". When applied, the principle constitutes "others" as of the same genus as X and Y, as opposed to giving it a far wider meaning encompassing things unrelated to X and Y.

In BII cases, a wording frequently arises in disease clauses by which insurers agree to provide cover if losses are suffered due to business interruption arising from "*the presence of vermin or defects in the drains or other sanitary arrangements at the Premises*". In the context of the pandemic, the only part of the clause which could, on a rather strained construction, encompass COVID-19 is the reference to "other sanitary arrangements". *Ejusdem generis*, however, constitutes "other sanitary arrangements" as of the same genus as matters relating to "vermin" and "drains" such that it could not be read as pertaining to anything connected with hygiene or sanitation. Instead, the principle would narrow its construction to things of the established genus, for example, leaks of sewage, woodworm infestation, blocked drains, legionella in pipes or other such things.

In *Thames & Mersey Marine v Hamilton Fraser (The Inchmaree)*[33], the clause was substantially wider than the above example:

> "LORD HALSBURY L.C.:— My Lords, in this case a policy of marine insurance for twelve months was effected upon, among other things, a pump on board the Inchmaree steamer. The adventures and perils which the capital stock and funds of the defendant company were made liable to by the policy of insurance were of the seas, men-of-war, fire, enemies, pirates, rovers, thieves, jettisons, letters of mart and countermart, surprisals, takings at sea, arrests, restraints and detainments of all kings, princes, and people of what nation, condition, or quality soever, barratry of the master and mariners, and of all other perils, losses, and

33 (1887) 12 App. Cas. 484.

> misfortunes that had or should come to the hurt, detriment, or damage of the aforesaid subject-matter of insurance or any part thereof."

In *The Inchmaree*, the court considered that the term "all other perils" ought not to include the explosion of a "donkey boiler" on board the vessel because the term was restricted to the same genus constituted by the other terms.

An important modern illustration in the context of business interruption insurance appears in *Tektrol*, where the claimant was the beneficiary of an "all risks" policy which excluded damage caused by, or consequential loss arising from "*erasure loss distortion or corruption of information on computer systems or other records programmes or software caused deliberately by rioters strikers locked-out workers persons taking part in labour disturbances or civil commotion or malicious persons*". The claimant's managing director received by e-mail a Christmas card attachment purportedly from a firm of solicitors, containing a computer virus. He opened the attachment, leading to the deletion of valuable source code and the company claimed for an indemnity under their insurance policy. As regards that exclusion, the Court of Appeal took the view that "malicious persons" did not include computer hackers because the preceding items in the list in the exclusion established a genus of actors which intended deliberate harm to the claimant specifically. "Malicious persons" therefore did not include computer hackers, who in the circumstances of the case, could only have intended harm to a class of persons rather than to the claimant specifically.

Also of interest in the judgment is the dissenting view of Carnwarth LJ, who, although he dissented on another issue, agreed with the majority on the interpretation of the above exclusion, and gave some guidance on the interpretation of "all risks" policies:

> "I have not found this an easy contract to construe. Although it is described as an "all risks" policy, one has to search long and hard, through a bewildering and apparently comprehensive list of exclusions, to discover the extent to which any risks are in fact covered. Mr Railton described the exclusion clauses as designed to "shape" the cover in

> respect of particular risks. I am prepared to assume that that was the intention, although it does not seem the most obvious drafting technique to achieve it. In any event, I agree with Buxton LJ that the exclusions should, where possible, be narrowly construed. One should start from the presumption that the parties intended an "all risks" policy to cover all risks, except when they are clearly and unambiguously excluded."

Noscitur a sociis

Closely related to the *ejusdem generis* principle is construction *noscitur a sociis*[34]- a maxim which emphasises the importance of context. The maxim dictates that words which are unclear, however general, must be interpreted according to those around them.

By way of example, the same policy in *Tektrol* provided another exclusion: for "*erasure loss distortion or corruption of information on computer systems*". A burglary (which sadly followed the computer virus in that case), meant that valuable source code on a company laptop was lost when the computer was stolen. The insurer sought to apply the exclusion on the basis that "loss" included the loss of information on a computer. Per Sir Martin Nourse:

> '"Loss" is a word whose meaning varies widely with the context in which it is used. If a man said to you: "I have lost my wife", you would understand him to mean one thing outside the maze at Hampton Court and another outside an undertakers in the high street.'

The majority of the Court of Appeal took the view that loss ought to be construed in the context of its surrounding words, such that loss was not a general term encompassing any type of loss, such as loss of data by

---

34 "known by its associates".

theft of the computer, but was instead limited to the sorts of loss described by the other words, i.e. erasure, distortion and corruption:

> "If, however, "loss" is read in its context, its meaning becomes plain. The expression "other erasure loss distortion or corruption of information" demonstrates that the loss contemplated is loss by means of electronic interference; *noscitur a sociis*. It is not just the effect of the other three words, but the order in which the four appear. "Loss" follows "erasure". While erasure can be expected to result in loss, a careful draftsman would not necessarily assume that it was the only way in which information might be lost. Then follow "distortion or corruption", which seem to refer to interference causing something less than erasure or loss and between which, as Lord Justice Buxton has observed, it is difficult to suggest a clear distinction. I agree with him that all four are overlapping words used by the draftsman to ensure that he had not omitted any case in which the information on the computer systems etc., was interfered with by electronic means."

Technical Words

Many BII policies contain lists of specified diseases. Some of those terms are more readily understandable: "Measles", "Rabies". Some are in less common use: "Ophthalmia neonatorum", "Haemolytic Uraemic Syndrome (HUS)". In deciding whether a particular disease, like COVID-19, is covered by the scope of the policy, it is worth considering what the listed terms mean, and what legal principles govern how the terms are to be construed.

In the case of *Rockliffe Hall v Travelers Insurance Company Ltd.*[35], the business interruption policy contained a number of diseases, ranging

35 [2021] EWHC 412 (Comm).

from the unspecific to the specific. The claim was pleaded on the basis that the list contained diseases which were both general in nature and specific in nature, and the court's opinion was sought on whether "Plague" meant the disease caused by the bacterium *Yersinia Pestis* or whether it was wider in meaning. Cockerill J was referred to a number of dictionary definitions, including medical dictionary definitions, which described the disease in two ways: either as that specific diseases, or "any epidemic disease with a high death rate".

The court's consideration of medical dictionaries has a long standing. Although technical or scientific terminology ought not to be construed in preference to commonly-accepted meaning, where that exists[36], the court is entitled to look at dictionaries and other materials to interpret the meaning of words, per Lord Hoffman in *Mannai Investment Co Ltd v Eagle Star Life Assurance Co Ltd*[37]:

> "The meaning of words, as they would appear in a dictionary, and the effect of their syntactical arrangement, as it would appear in a grammar, is part of the material which we use to understand a speaker's utterance. But it is only a part; another part is our knowledge of the background against which the utterance was made. It is that background which enables us, not only to choose the intended meaning when a word has more than one dictionary meaning but also, in the ways I have explained, to understand a speaker's meaning, often without ambiguity, when he has used the wrong words."

36 See, for example, "gas" and "fire", which have scientific meanings and commonly-understood meanings, *Re Hooley Hill Rubber & Chemical Co Ltd* [1920] 1 K.B. 257 and *Commonwealth Smelting v Guardian Royal Exchange* [1984] 2 Lloyd's Rep. 608.

37 [1997] A.C. 749.

CHAPTER SEVEN

CAUSATION

Of fundamental importance to all claims is the issue of causation and the way in which that was decided in FCA 1 and overruled in FCA 2. The decision on causation in FCA 2 has a substantial effect on the way in which varying policy wordings operate and also on how the court approaches "radius cases" as distinct from "at the premises" cases and "disease clauses" as distinct from "denial of access" clauses. In cases involving denial of access clauses, for example, insurers may well seek to argue that causation cannot be satisfied where policy wordings limit occurrences to being at the premises. It is therefore important to understand the fundamental difference in approach to causation between FCA 1 and FCA 2 and the effect of that on BII claims.

By way of example, insurers had frequently, in their earlier letters of declinature, refused to accept that the national lockdown was imposed "as a result of" a particular case within a radius of any particular business making the claim, but instead, in response to a national outbreak of COVID-19. The rationale behind their argument that was that many of the insurance policies were worded to make provision for closure relating to blockage of drains, outbreaks of *Legionella* or other such local perils which necessitated closure, and that more clear wording would have been required for cover to have been provided for national outbreaks of a disease.

The issue of causation was decided definitively by the UK Supreme Court in FCA 2. The legal argument on that point was complex, but the outcome of the decision was that what caused the lockdown, i.e. closure of any particular business, and therefore the business interruption losses, was any particular occurrence within the policy area along with all the other occurrences of COVID-19 across the UK as concurrent causes.

The decision was a move away from the "but for" test argued for by insurers and applied in FCA 1 (albeit in a composite manner as explained further below). The Supreme Court held:

> "212. We conclude that, on the proper interpretation of the disease clauses, in order to show that loss from interruption of the insured business was proximately caused by one or more occurrences of illness resulting from COVID-19, <u>it is sufficient to prove that the interruption was a result of Government action taken in response to cases of disease which included at least one case of COVID-19 within the geographical area covered by the clause</u>. The basis for this conclusion is the analysis of the court below, which in our opinion is correct, that each of the individual cases of illness resulting from COVID-19 which had occurred by the date of any Government action was a separate and equally effective cause of that action (and of the response of the public to it). Our conclusion does not depend on the particular terminology used in the clause to describe the required causal connection between the loss and the insured peril and applies equally whether the term used is "following" or some other formula such as "arising from" or "as a result of". It is a conclusion about the legal effect of the insurance contracts as they apply to the facts of this case."

<u>Causation in FCA 1</u>

The usual and familiar approach to causation is the "but for" test, i.e. "but for the particular event, a particular loss would not have happened". The insurers contended for a "but for" approach to causation in insurance cases and relied heavily on the decision of Hamblen J in *Orient-Express Hotels Ltd v Assicurazioni Generali SpA* [2010] EWHC 1186 (Comm); [2010] Lloyd's Rep IR 531.

Although there had been substantial criticism of the *Orient Express* case at the time of the decision in FCA 1, the court took the view that it did not provide an answer to the interpretation of clauses in the context of

BII as to how the "but for" test should be applied, because cases in the context of the pandemic involved composite or compound perils.

The court said this:

> "529. It follows that, if we had thought that the decision in *Orient Express* somehow dictated the consequences in terms of cover and the counterfactual analysis for which the insurers contend in the present case, we would have reached the conclusion that it was wrongly decided and declined to follow it. However, we do not need to go that far because even if *Orient Express* was correctly decided, it is clearly distinguishable from the present case in relation to those wordings which we have concluded provide cover in principle. *Orient Express* was simply not concerned with the type of insured perils involved here, including in particular the composite or compound perils which feature in many of the policies which we have had to consider, and nothing in the judge's analysis has any impact on the correct construction of the wordings we have been considering."

The court in FCA 1 adopted precisely the approach to causation which the above paragraph hinted at: that although the test was still "but for" causation, the question was "but for what?", and in the circumstances of the FCA litigation the "what" was not a single cause, i.e. a single case of COVID-19 occurring at particular premises, but a compound or combination of causes comprising localised cases and also those further afield taken together.

The court therefore held, at para. 530, that in relation to prevention of access clauses, the insured peril was a composite one involving interconnected elements:

> (i) prevention or hindrance of access to or use of the premises;
>
> (ii) by any action of government;

(iii) due to an emergency which could endanger human life and for cover to be triggered that composite insured peril must have caused the interruption or interference with the business.

In "hybrid" clauses, which involve closure as a result of disease within a policy area, the court defined the composite peril (see para. 531) as:

(i) inability to use the insured premises;

(ii) due to restrictions imposed by a public authority;

(iii) following the occurrence of a human infectious or contagious disease.

The effect of that was a significant win for businesses because the causation test was overcome without having to prove causation arising from solely a specific case of COVID-19 within the relevant policy area. Indeed, in concluding paragraph 351, the court added "*To the extent that any insured can show that there was a relevant restriction and an inability to use the premises, in assessing what loss the insured can recover, each of these interconnected elements should be removed from the counterfactual.*"

In relation to "disease clauses", the court adopted a similar approach (emphasis added):

> "Similarly, in relation to the disease clauses where we have concluded that there is cover in principle, we have done so because we consider that on the correct construction of those wordings, they insure the effects of COVID-19 both within the particular radius and outside it, the whole of the disease both inside and outside the relevant area has to be stripped out in the counterfactual. One of the fundamental fallacies in the insurers' approach is to treat the occurrence of COVID-19 within the relevant radius or "Vicinity" of the insured premises as completely separate from its occurrence elsewhere in the country as a whole."

The difficulty, however, with the approach in FCA 1 was that many clauses specifically required there to be an occurrence of COVID-19 within the policy area, and to frame causation in such a way as to exclude the individual elements of the composite test from the counterfactual, the claimant could get away without having to satisfy the requirements of the plain wording of the policy as to an "occurrence" of COVID-19 within the policy area being the cause of the insured loss. The insurers appealed.

Causation in FCA 2

Although the Supreme Court accepted that in relation to disease clauses such as RSA 3, as interpreted by court in FCA 1, questions of causation largely answered themselves, the Supreme Court took a very different of their interpretation and the relevant test on causation (see also para. 59 of FCA 2):

> "161. On what we consider to be the correct interpretation of the disease clauses, however, questions of causation are of crucial importance. We have concluded that the clauses cover only the effects of cases of COVID-19 occurring within the specified radius of the insured premises. On this basis, the question of what connection must be shown between any such cases of disease and the business interruption loss for which an insurance claim is made becomes critical."

Although the court in FCA 1 decided that the individual components of the composite cause could be removed from the counterfactual, the insurers argued before the Supreme Court that that could not be done without ignoring the wording of the policies[38], i.e. that the occurrence

38 See also para. 61 of the decision in FCA 2, where the Supreme Court criticised the Divisional Court's interpretation of the relevant policy wordings in ignoring the requirement that there had to be "an occurrence" within a relevant policy area: "*63. The way in which ... the*

of disease within a policy area *had to have* some effect on the action taken by the UK Government:

> "177. The principal ground on which the insurers resist this analysis is that it cannot be said that, but for any individual case of illness resulting from COVID-19, the Government measures would not have been taken. The insurers argue, as a central plank of their case on these appeals, that whatever the exact nature of the causal link required by each sample policy wording it is a minimum requirement of any causation test that the occurrence of the insured peril made a difference to the occurrence of loss: in other words, it is necessary to show, at a minimum, that the loss would not have been sustained but for the occurrence of the insured peril. Thus, MS Amlin, whose submissions on this issue were adopted by the other insurers, said in their written case:
>
> "The basic, fundamental, threshold test for any factual causation inquiry is the 'but for' test. X cannot be a cause of Y if Y would in any event have occurred irrespective of – but for – X.""

The principal criticism, however, of the application of the "but for" test in many insurance cases, was that it excludes a great many cases in which X would not be an effective or proximate cause of Y. The Supreme Court went on to give a number of examples:

1. Where a ship sinks and loses its cargo and the circumstances which may have given rise to that are numerous: the condition of the vessel, weather conditions, the decision to manufacture the vessel, the decision to deploy the vessel on its particular

---

FCA sought to defend the result reached by the court below involved interpreting the word "occurrence" to mean or be capable of meaning an "outbreak" of a Notifiable Disease. ... "

route, the buyer's decision to purchase the cargo and the seller's decision to ship the cargo on the particular vessel.

2. Where two fires[39] are started independently of each other which both combine to burn down a property and in which circumstances it is natural to regard both fires as causing the loss, but where it could not be said of each fire that but for it taking place, the loss would not have been caused.

3. Where two hunters simultaneously shoot a hiker[40] who is behind some bushes and medical evidence shows that either bullet would have killed the hiker instantly even if the other bullet had not been fired, such that application of the "but for" test strictly speaking would mean that neither shot caused the hiker's death, quite contrary to common-sense.

4. Where 20 individuals who all combine to push a bus over a cliff[41], and it is shown that only 13 or 14 people would have been needed to bring about that result. It could not then be said that the participation of any given individual was either necessary or sufficient to cause the destruction of the bus. Although it seems appropriate to describe each person's involvement as a cause of the loss, application of the "but for" test as a minimum threshold which must always be crossed if X is to be regarded as a cause of Y would again lead to the absurd conclusion that no one's actions caused the bus to be destroyed.

---

39 Hart and Honoré – Causation in the Law, 2nd ed (1985), p 206.

40 Supreme Court of Canada in *Cook v Lewis* [1951] SCR 830.

41 J Stapleton, "Unnecessary causes" (2013) 129 LQR 39; and "An 'extended but for' test for the causal relation in the law of obligations" (2015) 35 OJLS 697.

5. Where the directors of a company unanimously vote to put on the market a dangerous product[42] which causes injuries, although the decision only required the approval of a majority and it cannot be said that any individual director's vote was either necessary or sufficient to cause the product to be marketed and yet it is reasonable to regard each vote as causative rather than to say that none of the votes caused the decision to be made.

6. Where, in a similar vein to the examples above, multiple polluters discharge hazardous waste into a river.

The potential difficulty, raised by Professor Wright[43], with simply adopting an approach that recognises concurrent causes as in the above examples, however, is where the possible concurrent causes, as in the case of COVID-19 number in the many thousands, and it may not be appropriate to recognise trivial causative contributions to a result, such as the absurd examples given in para. 189 of FCA 2 like a teaspoonful of water contributing to a flooding river or a single match contributing to a raging forest fire. The court in FCA 2 did not agree, however, that a single answer could be given for all circumstances in which there may be contributing causes, and that the answer in such circumstances depended on the context in which the question was being considered (emphasis added):

> "190. We do not agree with Professor Wright in so far as he is suggesting in this passage that causation is a pure question of fact, albeit one that may be overlaid in areas such as tort and criminal law by questions of responsibility. <u>Whether an event which is one of very many that combine to cause loss should be regarded as a cause of the loss is not</u>

42 See para 185 of FCA 2.

43 RW Wright, "The NESS Account of Natural Causation: A Response to Criticisms" in R Goldberg (ed), Perspectives on Causation (Hart 2011) 285 at pp 304-305.

> a question to which any general answer can be given. It must always depend on the context in which the question is asked. Where the context is a claim under an insurance policy, judgements of fault or responsibility are not relevant. All that matters is what risks the insurers have agreed to cover. We have already indicated that this is a question of contractual interpretation which must accordingly be answered by identifying (objectively) the intended effect of the policy as applied to the relevant factual situation. "

The Supreme Court's view expressed at paragraph 190, crucially, formed the basis for the court's conclusion as to how concurrent causes in the case of COVID-19 ought to be treated- by construction of the policy in context: "*...For these reasons there is nothing in principle or in the concept of causation which precludes an insured peril that in combination with many other similar uninsured events brings about a loss with a sufficient degree of inevitability from being regarded as a cause – indeed as a proximate cause – of the loss, even if the occurrence of the insured peril is neither necessary nor sufficient to bring about the loss by itself...*".

The context of insurance policies providing cover for diseases like COVID-19, in the Supreme Court's view[44], required consideration of the nature of the diseases for which cover was being provided and the contracting parties' intentions. The court took the view that the sorts of diseases covered were known by the parties to sometimes spread rapidly, widely and unpredictably, such that no reasonable person could suppose that an outbreak could happen solely within a relevant policy area, nor that in the case of such outbreaks, the measures imposed by a public authority would be in response solely to one or other occurrence of disease within one or other relevant policy area.

---

44 Para 194 in FCA 2.

Having reached the view, therefore, that the policy wordings required there to be an occurrence within a particular policy area, overruling the Divisional Court on its decision on "composite causation", the Supreme Court held that application of the test for causation nevertheless allowed claimants to argue that their particular occurrence of COVID-19 along with all the other such cases was what caused the public authority intervention, and thus, taking with one hand and giving with the other, the Supreme Court set out the test for causation at para. 212.

CHAPTER EIGHT

DISEASE CLAUSES

Notifiable Diseases

The Health Protection (Notification) (Amendment) Regulations 2020/237 came into force on 5th March 2020 at 6:15am. They amended Schedules 1 and 2 of The Health Protection (Notification) Regulations 2010 ("the 2010 Regulations") to make COVID-19 a "notifiable disease" and SARS-Cov-2 a "notifiable causative agent".

The notification regulations provide a statutory framework for medical professionals to notify local authorities of cases of certain diseases. As set out at para. 2.1 of the Explanatory Memorandum to the Joint Committee on Statutory Instruments accompanying the legislation:

> "These Regulations create a scheme for notifying actual and suspected cases of infection and contamination in humans to specified bodies with public health responsibilities. This allows prompt action to be taken by those bodies to protect public health where appropriate."

Regulation 2 of the 2010 Regulations provides:

> "2.— **Duty to notify suspected disease, infection or contamination in patients**
>
> (1) A registered medical practitioner (R) must notify the proper officer of the relevant local authority where R has reasonable grounds for suspecting that a patient (P) whom R is attending—
>
> > (a) has a notifiable disease;
> >
> > (b) has an infection which, in the view of R, presents or could present significant harm to human health; or

> (c) is contaminated in a manner which, in the view of R, presents or could present significant harm to human health."

Schedule 1 of the 2020 Regulations contains a list of "notifiable diseases". Schedule 2 contains a list of notifiable "causative agents". The current Schedule 1 list reads (excerpt quoted):

> "Acute encephalitis
>
> Acute meningitis
>
> Acute poliomyelitis
>
> Acute infectious hepatitis
>
> Anthrax
>
> Botulism
>
> Brucellosis
>
> Cholera
>
> [COVID-19]
>
> Diphtheria
>
> Enteric fever (typhoid or paratyphoid fever)
>
> Food poisoning
>
> Haemolytic uraemic syndrome (HUS)
>
> Infectious bloody diarrhoea
>
> Invasive group A streptococcal disease and scarlet fever
>
> Legionnaires' Disease
>
> Leprosy
>
> Malaria
>
> Measles
>
> Meningococcal septicaemia

Mumps

Plague

Rabies

Rubella

SARS

…"

The current Schedule 2 list (excerpt quoted) reads:

"…

Mumps virus

Mycobacterium tuberculosis complex

Neisseria meningitidis

Omsk haemorrhagic fever virus

Plasmodium falciparum, vivax, ovale, malariae, knowlesi

Polio virus (wild or vaccine types)

Rabies virus (classical rabies and rabies-related lyssaviruses)

Rickettsia spp

Rift Valley fever virus

Rubella virus

Sabia virus

Salmonella spp

SARS coronavirus

[SARS-CoV 2]

Shigella spp

Streptococcus pneumoniae (invasive)

Streptococcus pyogenes (invasive)

Varicella zoster virus

Variola virus

Verocytotoxigenic Escherichia coli (including E.coli O157)

Vibrio cholerae

West Nile Virus

Yellow fever virus

Yersinia pestis"

Reference within Policy wordings

It is very common for BII policies to provide cover for "notifiable diseases". The RSA 3 example above does so by making reference to the statutory list of notifiable diseases:

> "**We** shall indemnify **You** in respect of interruption or interference with the **Business** during the **Indemnity Period** following:
>
> a) any
>
> i. occurrence of a Notifiable Disease (as defined below) at the **Premises** or attributable to food or drink supplied from the **Premises**;
>
> …
>
> Additional Definition in respect of Notifiable Diseases
>
> 1. Notifiable Disease shall mean illness sustained by any person resulting from:
>
> i. food or drink poisoning; or

> ii. any human infectious or human contagious disease excluding Acquired Immune Deficiency Syndrome (AIDS) or an AIDS related condition an outbreak of which the competent local authority has stipulated shall be notified to them..."

A key decision in FCA 1 arose from a point that at the time that most of the relevant insurance policies were concluded, COVID-19 had not been added to the statutory list and was therefore not then a notifiable disease. According to the usual approach to contractual interpretation, the court would have to be satisfied as to the objectively ascertainable intentions of the parties *at the time the contract was made,* such that COVID-19 would not have been included.

On one view, the parties were making reference to a statutory list knowing that the list could be altered from time to time, and indeed had been amended over the years. By reference to such a dynamic list, the parties, could arguably have been agreeing that cover would be provided for any disease currently listed or added later.

The court took the view that that was indeed the case, clarifying at paragraph 160 of the judgment, that it ought to be included despite it having been added later (emphasis added):

> "...Extension 4(d) was business interruption resulting from Notifiable Human Diseases, and that it was known at the time of the conclusion of the contracts that such diseases embraced the list to which we have already referred, including SARS and other highly contagious or infectious diseases, which were required to be notified precisely in order to permit a response from the authorities, and some of which were capable of spreading over large areas, as infected people moved around. *Furthermore, the nature of the definition of Notifiable Human Diseases in the policy meant that newly occurring diseases, if made notifiable by the relevant authorities, would count, even if they had not existed or been notifiable at the outset of the policy....*"

The point was not taken further in FCA 2 (emphasis added):

> "53. Three preliminary points may be made about this wording which are not in dispute. First, it is agreed that by 6 March 2020 COVID-19 had been designated in all parts of the United Kingdom as a disease which fell within the description in limb (ii) of the definition of a "Notifiable Disease" quoted above. The obligation to notify cases or suspected cases of certain diseases to the relevant local authority is not in fact (as the wording of the definition would suggest) a matter of stipulation by the local authority but, as mentioned earlier, is imposed by legislation. Nevertheless, a reasonable reader of the insurance policy who wanted to know whether a particular disease fell within limb (ii) of the definition of a "Notifiable Disease" would understand it as intended to refer to those diseases which are classified as "notifiable diseases" by the 2010 Regulations (and equivalent legislation for other parts of the UK). Second, in order for illness resulting from COVID-19 to be "sustained by any person" within the meaning of the "Notifiable Disease" definition, the court below found that it is not necessary for the person concerned to have been diagnosed as having the disease or to have manifested symptoms of illness: it is sufficient that the person should in fact have contracted the disease, whether or not the disease is symptomatic or has been diagnosed. The manifestation of symptoms and the making of a diagnosis are therefore relevant only to questions of proof. There is no challenge to that finding. Third, it is common ground that the word "following" at the end of the opening words of the insuring clause does not mean merely "later in time than" but requires there to be a causal connection between one of the perils specified in (a) to (d) and the interruption to the policyholder's business. There is a dispute about the precise nature of the required causal connection, to which we will return later in this judgment when we address questions of causation."

Lists of Diseases

In contrast to the straightforward reference to cover for "notifiable diseases", many policies import a list of diseases into the policy wording itself. The leading authority on lists of diseases is *Rockliffe Hall Ltd v Travelers Insurance Co Ltd*[45]. In that case, the policy did not use the term "notifiable disease", but instead used the term "Infectious Disease" and went on to provide a definition of that term within the policy as follows:

"Infectious Disease

Infectious Disease means

(i) Food or Drink poisoning

(ii) Cholera

Plague

Relapsing fever

Smallpox

Typhus

(iii) Acute encephalitis	Meningococcal septicaemia (without meningitis)
Acute poliomyelitis	Mumps
Anthrax	Ophthalmia neonatorum
Chicken Pox	Paratyphoid fever
Diphtheria	Rabies
Dysentery (amoebic or bacillary)	Rubella
Haemolytic Uraemic Syndrome (HUS)	Scarlet fever

45 [2021] EWHC 412 (Comm).

Infectious bloody diarrhoea	Tetanus
Invasive Group A streptococcal disease (GAS)	Tuberculosis
Leprosy	Typhoid fever
Leptospirosis	Viral haemorrhagic fever
Malaria	Viral hepatitis
Measles	Whooping cough
Meningitis	Yellow fever"

It appears that for no other reason than convenience, the vast majority of insurers, when deciding how to word their policies, either simply made reference to cover for "notifiable diseases" or, imported the then current Schedule 1 list directly into certain policies. Some insurers took the Schedule 1 list and modified it.

It is unclear why insurers including Travelers chose not to provide cover based on the more specific Schedule 2 list, nor why insurers used the Schedule 1 list in contexts other than those involving the identification of a particular case of a disease (i.e. the very purpose of the framework of the 2010 Regulations).

Rather than providing cover based on the occurrence of a specific case of a disease, the insurer in *Rockliffe* provided cover in circumstances where was is an "*An outbreak of an Infectious Disease within 10 miles of the Business Premises*".

According to the definition provided in the policy above, "Infectious Disease" includes both Acute encephalitis (swelling of the brain) and Malaria. A physician can presumably, in order to comply with reg. 2(1)(a) of the 2010 Regulations, identify whether "a patient has [swelling of the brain]" or "a patient has Malaria", but inclusion of the same list within a policy for which the condition of cover is an "outbreak" is problematic, because although one may have an outbreak of Malaria one cannot have an outbreak of swelling of the brain, any more than an outbreak of swelling of the knee.

That absurdity arises from the fact that many of the notifiable diseases have the same name as their relevant notifiable causative agent, but for some diseases the causative agent has an unintuitive name, and there does not appear to be any express way to link specific items on the Schedule 1 and Schedule 2 lists, other than by implication.

In *Rockliffe*, the Claimant pleaded the unworkability of the list in the following way, making reference to the inclusion of diseases which were ambiguous, but also that the nature of the list itself was ambiguous[46]:

> "**E. The Disease Clause**
>
> 24. The list of diseases defined within the term "Infectious Diseases", as set out above, includes diseases with multiple causes, such as "Food or Drink poisoning", "Plague", "Acute encephalitis", "Viral Hepatitis" and "Meningitis" ("**General Diseases**").
>
> 25. The Claimant avers that such General Diseases do not define which causative agents, conditions, or pathogens were intended to trigger cover.
>
> 26. The list also includes within the term "Infectious Diseases" diseases with single, identifiable or specific causes, such as "Rabies", "Malaria" and "Anthrax" ("**Specific Diseases**").
>
> 27. The list is therefore a mixture of General Diseases and Specific Diseases.
>
> **Ambiguous/General Diseases**
>
> 28. The Claimant avers that on a proper construction of the Disease Clause:

---

46 See Particulars of Claim in *Rockliffe*.

(a) COVID-19 falls within the definition of "Plague", which is not limited by the wording of the clause to the variety of diseases caused by the bacterium *Yersinia Pestis*;

(b) COVID-19 also falls within the definition of "Food or Drink poisoning", "Acute encephalitis", "Viral Hepatitis" and "Meningitis" or any such General Disease within the list, if such General Disease is capable of, or likely to be caused by Coronavirus infection and/or associated with COVID-19.

29. The Claimant further claims that such General Diseases are at the very least ambiguous in their definition and ought to be construed *Contra Proferentem* against the Defendant, such General Diseases having been drafted by the Defendant as part of its standard form of policy and the Claimant therefore claims a declaration in the terms set out in paragraph 28 above.

Ambiguous/General List

30. The Claimant avers that on a proper construction of the Disease Clause, it cannot be limited solely to specific diseases caused by specific causative agents, conditions or pathogens because the list of Infectious Diseases includes both General Diseases and Specific Diseases.

31. The Claimant therefore avers that the list of Infectious Diseases is general in nature and/or unclear/ambiguous, on a literal reading of it, as to which causative agents, conditions or pathogens were intended to cause any of the General Diseases and therefore form the basis for cover under the terms of the Policy.

32. The Claimant therefore avers that on a proper construction of the Disease Clause, the list of Infectious Diseases intended to trigger it included:

(a) any Specific Diseases included on the list; and/or

(b) any disease, taking into account all the circumstances, bearing a reasonable similarity to any of the General Diseases or Specific Diseases set out on the list.

33. Without prejudice to the arguments in paragraphs 28 and 29 above, the Claimant further avers that COVID-19 bears a reasonable similarity in all the circumstances to the diseases listed and on a proper construction of the Disease Clause and list of Infectious Diseases is capable of triggering cover under the Disease Clause.

34. The Claimant further claims that the list of Infectious Diseases is at the very least ambiguous in its scope and ought to be construed Contra Proferentem against the Defendant, such list having been drafted by the Defendant as part of its standard form of policy.

Ambiguity/Generality of the List

The argument in *Rockliffe* as to the nature of the list put forward the proposed test in para. 32(b) of the above pleading as the only sensible interpretation of the list, i.e. as an *indicative* list which would have excluded trivial or dissimilar illnesses, but included illnesses similar enough on the evidence to those in the list. The argument sought to rely on the fact that a number of the listed diseases were effectively meaningless in the context of an outbreak, and only had meaning in the context of identification of a specific case of a disease, or put another way: that whilst one can have a case of encephalitis (swelling of the brain), one cannot have an *outbreak* of encephalitis, because encephalitis is a symptom of a causative factor, not the causative factor itself. Further, in the case of encephalitis and others, the causes of that symptom were many, being caused by various bacteria, viruses, or genetic conditions.

The argument also suggested that there was little or no difference between making reference to an external dynamic list, and importing that dynamic list into the policy wording. The Claimant sought to argue that there was therefore an analogy to be drawn with the court's decision in FCA 1 when it defined what "notifiable disease" meant. The rationale for the court's conclusion was that the nature of the diseases listed was such that the parties, by making reference to a list of diseases which could spread widely and were sufficient to merit a response by local authorities in implementing public health measures, intended to agree cover for similar sorts of diseases which would be added to the list later.

Cockerill J rejected those arguments, concluding that the reference to "*Specified Disease means*" instead created a static list which defined the scope of cover- there was therefore no basis for arguing that the list, because of its similarity to the Schedule 1 list, was capable of including COVID-19:

> "84. It is therefore clear that the Notifiable Diseases clause in that case made explicit reference to an externally maintained and dynamic list regularly updated by the UK Government. There is no such reference here. The Policy in this case takes a very different approach setting out its own static list including only a limited list of the diseases that were known to the parties at the time. That list does not include diseases that are subsequently discovered, for the simple reason that they are not on the list. There is no future-looking "catch-all" wording. Thus whilst a "catch-all" "Notifiable Diseases" clause is (depending on its wording) likely to be inclusive of diseases which are added (after the time of contracting) to the statutory list of "Notifiable Diseases", a defined list of diseases is not."

Ambiguity/Generality of Diseases

The other of the alternative cases in *Rockliffe* was that even if the list were to be construed as a static list, defining the scope of cover, there were some diseases on the list which were not only general enough to include COVID-19 on the evidence, but were vague enough to allow construction *contra proferentem* in favour of the Claimant.

The Claimant referred to publicly available medical evidence, and sought to obtain expert evidence if the matter progressed further than the summary judgment stage, that there was a strong association between COVID-19 and, in particular, acute encephalitis. The fact that the medical dictionaries defined encephalitis as widely as they do also supported, it was argued, for the contention that the term ought to be construed *contra proferentem* to include COVID-19.

The judge rejected that argument on the basis that effectively COVID-19 was not synonymous with encephalitis and that even if COVID-19 did cause encephalitis it caused it only in a small number of cases:

> "72. The first approach would be to contend that Covid-19 is a form of meningitis or acute encephalitis, such that a diagnosis of Covid-19 is in fact a diagnosis of encephalitis and/or meningitis. That is not a tenable construction of the words. The reasonable person in the position of the parties would not understand these diseases to refer to Covid-19, which is a new disease (discovered after the Policy incepted), with a different name and commonly associated with entirely different main symptoms, definition and categorisation. If Covid-19 results in encephalitis or meningitis it plainly only does so in a small minority of cases. It would be an Alice in Wonderland approach to call Covid-19 "encephalitis" or "meningitis"."

Definition of "Plague"

Also of note was the court's determination as to whether "Plague" by definition included COVID-19. The court was referred to dictionary definitions in the Oxford English Dictionary and medical dictionaries which defined plague as meaning "any epidemic disease with a high death rate". Other definitions defined plague as meaning the disease caused by the bacterium *Yersinia Pestis*.

The argument put forward by the Claimant was that at the very least the term was ambiguous in that there were two definitions in general use: one which was very wide and one which was specific, such that the policy-holder should be given the benefit of the doubt *contra proferentem*.

The court rejected that argument on the basis that there was no genuine ambiguity, the current meaning being commonly-understood to be caused by *Yersinia Pestis*. The court was not persuaded that other policy wordings which made specific reference to the bubonic, pneumonic or septicaemic forms of the disease altered that interpretation.

SARS and SARS-Cov-2

A number of policies which contain a list of diseases list "SARS" as one of the diseases. There is no current authority which defines the term in this context, although it is to be noted that the term already appears in the Schedule 1 list of notifiable diseases under the 2010 Regulations.

As set out in FCA 1, the term SARS (Severe Acute Respiratory Syndrome) ordinarily refers to the 2002/2003 outbreak of SARS-Cov-1 in Asia. The causative agent of COVID-19 is SARS-Cov-2, which suggests at least on the face of it a different agent from that which caused "SARS" in the 2002/2003 context. Based on the logic in *Rockliffe*, the term SARS would probably not include COVID-19 on the basis that it is commonly understood to relate to the 2003 outbreak, however, that entails no consideration of the similarities and differences between SARS-Cov-1 and SARS-Cov-2 and the 2003 outbreak cannot, of course, happen in exactly the same way again. Nevertheless, many policies do provide cover for "SARS" and it is worth considering what parties may have intended that to cover. If they were providing cover only for the virus SARS-Cov-1, rather than SARS more generally, that does not appear in most policies to have been specified, and the commercial purpose of such a distinction is unclear, because, conceivably, the effects of SARS-Cov-1 may have been as much to do with the circumstances of the outbreak as the nature of the virus itself.

If the court is not concerned with the similarities or differences between the actual agents giving rise to business interruption, but more the labels by which such agents become known, then the commercial purpose of such policies could conceivably depend on the labels by which agents become known, and, had COVID-19 become known as "SARS 2", such an approach could, perhaps perversely, lead to a stronger argument for cover. If the court were minded to consider the agents themselves, expert evidence would no doubt be required on the issue of how such agents are named, what the similarities and differences in structure, infectiousness and mortality are and how substantial a mutation of such a virus has to be before it merits classifying it as a new agent, with a new name.

Manifestation

One of the most frequent questions arising in the context of the initial outbreak in the UK is how businesses go about proving whether COVID-19 actually occurred, a task made all the more difficult by the absence of any reliable testing regime at the time of the outbreak.

In FCA 1, the court adopted a wide definition of manifestation and made clear that a positive diagnosis is not required (see para. 53 dealt with more fully below). In the context of the QBE 1 policy wording, which required "manifestation" the court gave helpful guidance at para. 224 (emphasis added):

> "224. One minor issue of construction should be addressed at the outset. This is what is meant by "manifested" as used within Clause 7.3.9(a). Clearly someone who is displaying symptoms of a disease can be said to "manifest" it. We consider that it would also be the case that a person "manifested" the disease if, though superficially asymptomatic, he or she was diagnosed with the disease, because the disease would have "manifested" itself to the diagnoser. We do not consider that it is possible to speak of someone who is asymptomatic and has not been diagnosed as having the disease as having "manifested" it."

The above statement is not much more than a reference to the of the sort of evidence required to satisfy the ordinary civil burden of proof, which imposes no specific requirement for proof of a specific kind. Indeed, as to the issue of prevalence more generally the starting-point is consideration of the civil burden of proof: the way in which facts are proved in civil proceedings is by convincing the judge hearing the case at trial that something was "more likely than not to have happened". That is sometimes rephrased as "whether something probably happened". That is because the civil standard of proof is proof "on the balance of probabilities".

Although symptoms of manifestation by an individual, or a diagnosis, will likely satisfy the burden of proof, there are conceivably other ways in which the burden could be satisfied, and the FCA sought guidance from the court on what those might be.

The court in FCA 1, however, declined to give a definitive ruling on what evidence ought to be used to prove an occurrence of COVID-19 perhaps because such matters of proof are more usually left to the trial judge, but it did nevertheless give consideration to a number of types of evidence which could satisfy the burden (emphasis added):

> "Conclusions as to prevalence
>
> 567. <u>It is not possible for us to provide any generally applicable guidance as to what evidence may prove actual prevalence in varying factual contexts and for the purposes of different policies.</u> For example, some policies have a relevant policy area of 3.14 square miles (in the case of a one mile radius) and others have a relevant policy area of 1,963.5 square miles (in the case of a 25 mile radius). The relevant evidence as to prevalence will also vary according to the particular timing and location of the claim. And different inferences might be drawn from a combination of underlying data in different contexts.
>
> 568. The <u>two questions</u> which the Court has to consider at the general level are: <u>(1) what types of evidence could be used in principle to discharge the burden of proof on the insured as to prevalence</u>, and <u>(2) whether, assuming the FCA's evidence to be the best available evidence, that would be enough to discharge the burden of proof.</u>

...

Types of evidence

569. As to the first question, the insurers have conceded that the categories of evidence pleaded, that is, specific evidence, NHS Deaths Data, ONS Deaths Data and reported cases, are in principle capable of demonstrating the presence of COVID-19. They also accept that other types of statistical evidence could be used, as long as they are reliable. The issues between the parties are really to do with what inferences can be drawn from the available types of evidence, particularly as to the timing of the presence of the disease, and the use of data aggregated by reference to geographical areas which are not the same as the relevant policy areas. These are matters which as we see it can only be definitively determined at the level of individual claims, but some points can be made."

In paragraph 569, the court gave examples of relevant types of evidence:

1. specific evidence (i.e. diagnoses or symptoms);
2. NHS deaths data;
3. ONS deaths data;
4. reported cases;
5. other statistical evidence.

By "policy area", the court in FCA 1 was talking about clauses which often specify a radius within which a disease must occur in order for cover to be provided. Many types of clause provide geographical areas of "25 miles" or "5 miles", for example. In those circumstances where a large radius is defined it ought to be fairly easy to fulfil the FCA 2 causation test of proving an occurrence of COVID-19 within that radius. That was contemplated by the court in FCA1:

> "Specific evidence
>
> 542. First, and least contentiously, there may be specific evidence of a case or cases in a particular location within the relevant policy area. The example given by the FCA is "widespread reports that the care home down the road from the policyholder's premises has been the location of an outbreak of COVID-19". The insurers accepted in principle that an insured might be able to prove a case of COVID-19 at a particular location by specific evidence in a particular case, but submitted that it depends on an assessment of the relevant evidence in each case."

The task is somewhat more complicated where clauses specify that disease must have occurred "at the premises". Although the court did not specifically deal with "at the premises cases", there is no reason in principle why the same approach as applies to proof in radius cases cannot apply to proving occurrence at the premises. There was nothing in FCA 1 nor FCA 2 to fundamentally distinguish "at the premises" cases from "radius cases", and there is unlikely to be any logical basis for doing so: some clauses, for example, specify the policy area to be a radius of "1 mile" from the premises. In the case of a large shopping centre or golf-club, it could be that the curtilage of the premises extends beyond the distances sometimes specified in radius cases.

In principle, therefore, whilst direct evidence of COVID-19 occurring at the premises would be the strongest evidence, the indirect evidence in the form of NHS, ONS, and under-counting statistics discussed in FCA1 could equally apply to premises which are either large or have a high foot-fall.

In both "radius cases" and "at the premises" cases, therefore, it is important to consider the types of specific evidence, and indirect evidence which may satisfy the burden of proof.

Specific Evidence

As mentioned above, regarding manifestation, it is not necessary to provide a diagnosis of COVID-19.

The court in FCA 1 adopted a fairly wide definition of "manifestation" and that was affirmed at paragraph 53 by the court in FCA 2 (emphasis added):

> "Second, in order for illness resulting from COVID-19 to be "sustained by any person" within the meaning of the "Notifiable Disease" definition, <u>the court below found that it is not necessary for the person concerned to have been diagnosed as having the disease or to have manifested symptoms of illness</u>: it is sufficient that the person should in fact have contracted the disease, whether or not the disease is symptomatic or has been diagnosed. The manifestation of symptoms and the making of a diagnosis are therefore relevant only to questions of proof. There is no challenge to that finding."

Insurers have often adopted approaches to claims handling which require disclosure of specific documentary evidence at the initial stages of claims. For many businesses, records relating to staff absence will exist, as will sick notes, or e-mails between employer and employee relating to symptoms suffered. In businesses which deal with members of the public more generally, such as childcare businesses, GP practices, or similar, there will be records specific to individual members of the public which may refer to symptoms.

Even in the absence of such records, or indeed a diagnosis, in theory a credible witness statement from one or more people who either suffered symptoms, or who saw or were aware of others suffering symptoms around the time of the relevant lockdown would be sufficient to satisfy the burden of proof for manifestation in "at the premises" cases.

In radius cases, claimants may be able to look further afield, for example, press reports relating to care homes, hospitals or clinics within the relevant policy area.

Indirect Evidence

As above, the court will not limit claimants to only specific evidence of manifestation at the premises or in radius cases and has indicated that in principle that a claimant could adopt a methodology of proof by statistical means. That is not, however, to say that claimants are bound to go down the path of indirect evidence to the exclusion of specific evidence and claimants will, it is assumed, resort to various combinations of the two. A particular case might, for example, rely on evidence of one or more employees having COVID-19 symptoms (even absent a diagnosis) prior to the lockdown, in an NHS area which had a high number of cases, where the business was a pub or restaurant with a high foot-fall, all of which would combine to help satisfy the judge at trial.

The approach to indirect evidence was summarised by the court in FCA 1 with the agreement of the main insurers and at para. 579 (emphasis added):

> "579. In substance, what the FCA seeks in this case is reassurance that the types of methodologies it has suggested (in the form of averaging and undercounting) could in principle discharge the burden of proof. But that much has already been conceded. <u>The insurers have conceded that a distribution-based analysis, or an undercounting analysis, could in principle be used to discharge the burden of proof on an insured.</u> The insurers have accepted that insureds can seek to rely on the specific reports identified in this case. Unlike the defendants in Equitas, the insurers do not suggest that absolute precision is required and that otherwise the claims will fail. The real issues between the parties were as to the reliability of the particular methodologies introduced by the FCA. The parties were given an opportunity to pursue an additional trial in early September to deal with these matters but the FCA decided (perhaps understandably given the time- compressed nature of the July trial) to proceed with the questions as framed. The concessions which have been made by the insurers are important. <u>It is our hope and expectation that in the light of them insurers will be able to agree on any issues of prevalence which actually arise and are relevant to</u>

> particular cases. Further than that, however, we are not able to go."

As to the methodology of proof by indirect or statistical means, it is obvious that that will be far easier in "radius cases" where the clause requires proof of COVID-19 within a radius of 25 miles of the premises, which may well encompass a local general hospital or care home and will provide an easy factual basis for proving the presence of COVID-19.

Proof by such statistical methods becomes more difficult the smaller the radius is, simply for practical reasons, because there are fewer people within the radius and there is a lower probability of hospitals or other focal points for manifestation of the disease, but it ought not to be impossible to prove the occurrence of COVID-19 "at the premises" by statistical means albeit in the case of small premises with a low foot-fall that will be difficult compared to large premises open to the public for the same reason that a 1-mile radius provision would present more practical difficulties in proving the presence of COVID-19 than a large radius provision.

The court in FCA1 discussed the various types of proof (emphasis added) and proof of prevalence was not challenged in FCA 2 (see paras 46 and 47 of FCA 2):

> "The types of proof
>
> 541. The FCA submitted that there are four types of evidence which are sufficient in principle to discharge the burden of proof on an insured as to the prevalence of COVID- 19 in what it refers to as a "relevant policy area". These categories of evidence are described below, together with the relevant concessions made by the insurers.
>
> ...

NHS Deaths Data

The NHS has, since towards the beginning of the outbreak, published data on deaths in the UK. That is available online at https://www.england.nhs.uk/statistics/statistical-work-areas/covid-19-daily-deaths/

The significance of that data, as described by the court in FCA 1, is that, although it may not be informative as to the specific cause of death of a particular patient, it is nevertheless useful to show whether COVID-19 was present at a particular hospital (on the balance of probabilities) and therefore that may very well assist in satisfying the civil burden of proof if the hospital is within the policy area (emphasis added):

> "543. ... there are publicly available data published by NHS England which record the number of individuals who died in hospitals in England after having tested positive for COVID-19 ("NHS Deaths Data"). The NHS Deaths Data have been published on a daily basis and include data from 1 March 2020 onwards, showing both daily and cumulative totals, aggregated at the level of NHS Hospital Trusts. The FCA accepted that the NHS Deaths Data do not show the numbers of deaths caused by COVID-19 because, for example, an individual might test positive for COVID-19, but then recover and die in hospital from a different cause. The FCA submitted that this possibility does not affect the utility of the NHS Deaths Data in showing the presence of COVID-19 in a particular area. The FCA submitted that if a person contracted COVID-19 and then subsequently died from another cause, that makes no difference to the fact that COVID- 19 was present in the relevant NHS Hospital Trust at a time prior to the death. In other words, identifying the cause of individual deaths is not necessary for the purposes of proving prevalence.
>
> 544. As noted above, the NHS Deaths Data are aggregated at the level of NHS Hospital Trusts, each of which may contain more than one hospital. There may be situations

> where one of the Trust hospitals is within the relevant policy area whereas others are outside it. The parties were agreed that if there was at least one death in an NHS Hospital Trust, where there was only one hospital in that NHS Hospital Trust, and that hospital was within the relevant policy area, this would show the death of a person or persons who previously tested positive for COVID-19 within the relevant policy area. Similarly, if there was at least one death in a particular NHS Hospital Trust and all the hospitals in that NHS Hospital Trust were within the relevant policy area, this would show the death of a person or persons who had previously tested positive for COVID-19 within the relevant policy area."

ONS Deaths Data

The Office for National Statistics also publishes data on deaths due to COVID-19, which is available online at https://www.ons.gov.uk/peoplepopulationandcommunity/healthandsocialcare/conditionsanddiseases

The difference between ONS Deaths Data and NHS Deaths Data is that it is likely to indicate cause of death and the ONS also provides doctors with specific guidance on completing the "cause of death" section death certificates[47] in cases of COVID-19. The "cause of death" section of the certificate follows a well-understood scheme by which the sequence of causes of death is listed. In part 4.1 of the guidance, it says:

> "The MCCD in use in England and Wales currently has 3 lines in part I for the sequence leading directly to death. If you want to include more than 3 steps in the sequence, you

47 https://assets.publishing.service.gov.uk/government/uploads/system/uploads/attachment_data/file/877302/guidance-for-doctors-completing-medical-certificates-of-cause-of-death-covid-19.pdf

can do so by writing more than one condition on a line, indicating clearly that one is due to the next.

> Example:
>
> Ia. Post-transplant lymphoma
>
> Ib. Immunosuppression following renal transplant 15 years ago
>
> Ic. Glomerulonephrosis due to insulin dependent diabetes mellitus
>
> II. Recurrent urinary tract infections
>
> Insulin dependent diabetes with renal complications is the underlying cause."

The guidance also makes clear that "*COVID-19 is an acceptable direct or underlying cause of death for the purposes of completing the Medical Certificate of Cause of Death*" and so use of ONS Data on recorded deaths may arguably not only amount to indirect evidence suggesting that COVID-19 was likely to have manifested within a policy area, but also that in specific cases it did in fact manifest.

The court in FCA 1 summarised its view on what might be made of ONS Deaths Data at paras 545 to 547 (emphasis added):

> 545. … there are publicly available data published by the Office of National Statistics ("ONS") as to deaths which occurred each week in England and Wales. These statistics include deaths where the death involves COVID-19 on the basis that the death certificate mentions COVID-19 ("ONS Deaths Data"). The ONS Deaths Data are published on a weekly basis and are aggregated at the level of local authority or health board. <u>Unlike the NHS Deaths Data, there is no dispute that the ONS Deaths Data indicate deaths where the cause of death involved COVID-19</u>.

546. The insurers accept that an insured can prove the presence of at least one case of COVID-19 within a relevant policy area in a particular week if the ONS Deaths Data showed at least one death during that week within the local authority or health board, and that local authority or health board was entirely within the relevant policy area. There was disagreement, however, as to situations where the relevant policy area did not neatly correspond with the local authority or health board. In such cases, the FCA submitted an "averaging methodology" could be used to extrapolate the number of deaths in the relevant policy area. We discuss the use of an averaging methodology further below.

547. The insurers did not accept that the ONS Deaths Data could, on its own, show the presence of COVID-19 within the relevant policy area on any particular day of that week. But nonetheless the parties agreed that in principle if the ONS Deaths Data showed at least one death in a particular week in a relevant policy area, then it could be inferred that there was at least one case of COVID-19 in the period "immediately prior" to that week. The insurers submitted that the length of that period was not something the Court could decide without expert evidence.

Reported cases

The UK Government also provides data of reported numbers of cases of COVID-19 based on lab-test results at https://coronavirus.data.gov.uk/details/cases which is viewable across the country or by region.

The data on reported cases is of significance to claimants because although it might not show that there was a specific case of COVID-19 at business premises or within a relevant policy area, one might seek to infer from the rate of COVID-19 infections in a particular local authority or other area that there was a greater than 50% of COVID-19 manifesting within the relevant policy area, for example, if that policy area falls entirely or largely within a reporting area in which COVID-19 positive test results are high.

The Supreme Court analysed the utility of such evidence at paras. 548 to 551 (emphasis added):

> "548. … and perhaps most obviously, there are publicly available data as to the numbers of lab-confirmed positive tests of COVID-19 across the UK ("reported cases"). Daily and cumulative totals of reported cases have been published by the UK Government and are available online. The reported cases for each day originate from the testing of specimens taken in the previous few days. The parties agreed that data from around 5 days before can be considered complete. The reported cases can be aggregated across nations, regions, Upper Tier Local Authorities ("UTLAs") and Lower Tier Local Authorities ("LTLAs"). The allocation of a case to an area is done by reference to the home postcode of the individual who tested positive, established by ONS geographical area codes.
>
> 549. The insurers conceded that the reported cases on a particular date could demonstrate the presence of COVID-19 in a particular nation, region, UTLA or LTLA on that date. The relevance of cumulative totals was in dispute, however, because, as the FCA acknowledged, cumulative totals make no allowance for those who have recovered. The parties did agree, however, that a person will be infectious for a period of time, estimated to be 7-12 days in moderate cases and up to 14 days on average in severe cases. The FCA therefore submitted that an insured should not be limited to reliance on daily reported cases alone.
>
> 550. The most granular breakdown of daily and cumulative reported cases is at the level of LTLAs, of which there are 317 in England. A relevant policy area may overlap with LTLAs in different ways. The clearest case is where an LTLA is entirely within a relevant policy area. The parties agreed that an insured can prove the presence of at least one

> case of COVID-19 within a relevant policy area on a particular date if, on that date, the daily reported cases for the relevant LTLA are at least one and the LTLA is entirely within the relevant policy area. Whether the insured premises are within the boundary of the LTLA is neither here nor there.
>
> 551. In other cases, the relevant policy area might cover more than one LTLA. This is to be expected in the case of relevant policy areas with a 25 mile radius. The parties agreed that in such cases, an insured can prove the presence of at least one case of COVID-19 within the relevant policy area on a particular date if the daily reported cases for any one of the LTLAs in the relevant policy area is at least one, so long as that LTLA is entirely within the relevant policy area. Again, whether the insured premises are within the boundary of the LTLA is neither here nor there.

Other statistical methodologies

Claimants are entitled to rely on other statistical methodologies in order to prove the occurrence of cases within a relevant policy area. The FCA sought clarification on the use of such methodologies because it was conceivable that claimants may very well not be able to satisfy the burden solely by use of the types of evidence set out above.

Like with the other types of evidence, claimants will be entitled to rely on statistical proof along with the other types of evidence above.

The court summarised the main two types of statistical evidence, but the list is not exhaustive (emphasis added):

> "552. ... the FCA relied on certain methodologies which it submitted could be used by insureds, in conjunction with the available types of evidence identified above, to prove the prevalence of the disease... The first is the use of averages to determine prevalence in a relevant policy area, when the LTLA (or other area for which data are available) is not entirely within that relevant policy area. The second

> is attempting to establish an "undercounting ratio" to extrapolate the extent to which actual cases of COVID-19 exceeded the reported figures in particular areas and across the UK and using an "uplift" to accommodate for this."

Averaging methodology

The use of averaging methodologies is likely to be of use where policy areas do not fall entirely within a particular local authority area: it may well be partly within and partly outside, or where other evidence is difficult to obtain.

The approach to the population-weighted averaging methodology was fairly simple and the court gave an example of the type of methodology was provided at paragraph 555 in FCA 2:

1. Assume "Area A" has 100 cases of COVID-19 and a population of 50,000.

2. The relevant policy area, "Area B" has a population of 5,000.

3. Assume Area B is entirely within Area A.

4. The weighted averaging methodology extrapolates that Area B has 10 cases.

The illustration of that approach given at para. 555 was:

> "If the policyholder wished to take (say) 16 March 2020 as the relevant date for making a claim: in Cornwall as at 16 March 2020, there was a total of 14 cumulative Reported Cases …. The population of Cornwall based on the 2011 census was 532,273; and the population of a 25-mile Relevant Policy Area from the above postcode is approximately (based on public tools as to postcode populations) 350,000. That would amount to approximately 9-10 cases in the Relevant Policy Area."

The same approach could potentially be used where the relevant policy area crosses different local authority areas by using the methodology to extrapolate the likely number of cases in areas comprising the relevant policy area. The exercise is clearly more difficult in those circumstances and ought to take into account a number of different circumstances so as to amount to a reliable averaging methodology, and, no doubt, an expert report would be required to inform the court at trial as to what the likely chance was of a COVID-19 case existing within a relevant policy area at the relevant time. The court summarised the parties' arguments in relation to such methodologies as follows:

> "553. The parties did not reach agreement in relation to situations where the relevant policy area is partly within and partly outside a particular LTLA, or where the relevant policy area is entirely within an LTLA. The FCA submitted that in such cases the insured should in principle be able to use an "averaging methodology" to establish the number of cases in a relevant policy area. The FCA put forward the same methodology in respect of ONS Deaths Data.
>
> 554. The averaging methodology initially proposed by the FCA was to calculate the average number of cases or deaths per square mile in a region, and to use that average to show that there was at least one case in a relevant policy area within that region. This proposal was then qualified by reference to population weighting. The weighted averaging methodology calculates the ratio between: (1) the population of the relevant policy area; and (2) the population of the relevant region for which data are available. The FCA submitted that the populations of different areas could be calculated by reference to publicly available data, including at the level of postcodes and higher level census data. The ratio could then be used to extrapolate the number of deaths or cases in the relevant policy area.
>
> ...

> 556. The insurers accepted that in principle "some reliable method of calculating the distribution of cases across an area could be used". But they submitted that any averaging method would have to take into account context-specific factors and could be a complex task. Simple averages across areas were unlikely to be reliable or accurate, particularly across different types of area, for example where a relevant policy area was made up partly of major cities and partly of other rural areas. Population-weighted averages were also said to be unreliable because they assumed an even distribution across the population of a region, rather than considering other factors such as age, ethnicity, socioeconomic factors or concentrations near care homes. The insurers also submitted that, in any case, the Court was in no position to decide whether these particular averaging methods were reliable without expert evidence on the issue.

Undercounting

The basis of the undercounting methodology was the parties' agreement in FCA 1 that the actual presence of COVID-19 in the UK was likely to have been much higher than what was reflected in the numbers of reported cases, although the parties were unable to agree as to the extent of that difference.

The methodology seeks to apply an "undercounting ratio" with which to multiply the numbers of actual cases, to give a likely more accurate number of cases in the relevant policy area:

> 557. The parties agreed that the actual presence of COVID-19 in the UK in March 2020 would have been "much higher" than was reflected in the number of reported cases. However, the extent of the difference was not agreed. The FCA submitted that an insured should be able to rely on an appropriate "undercounting ratio" to extrapolate the actual prevalence of the disease in a given area (and then apply the averaging methodologies as required to show prevalence in a relevant policy area).

558. The FCA pointed to certain publicly available reports which modelled estimated infections at various points in time in the UK in order to support its argument about an undercounting ratio. The first was prepared by Imperial College London: Flaxman, S. et al, Report 13: Estimating the number of infections and the impact of non-pharmaceutical interventions on COVID-19 in 11 European countries (30 March 2020). The second is a series of reports prepared by the University of Cambridge: Birrell, P. et al, COVID-19: Nowcast and Forecast. These reports suggest significant undercounting in reported cases, including to the extent that reported cases may have reflected only 0.5% of actual cases at certain dates and in certain areas.

559. Given that the Court did not receive any expert evidence on the issue, there is little that it is possible or appropriate for us to say about the reports in terms of assessing their reliability. However, in its amended pleading, the FCA put its case as follows: "The true number of individuals infected with COVID-19 on relevant dates in March 2020 in a regional, UTLA or LTLA Zone can reasonably be estimated as the number of cases derived by applying an appropriate Undercounting Ratio for the relevant regional Zone to the Reported Cases in the regional Zone (or any UTLA or LTLA Zone within the regional Zone as appropriate), and an appropriate Undercounting Ratio can properly be inferred from the Imperial Analysis, the Cambridge Analysis or another relevant publicly available analysis from a suitably qualified institution."

560. The FCA submitted that the question for the Court was therefore whether this type of evidence – being evidence about undercounting which was relevant and from a suitably qualified institution – would prima facie be sufficient to discharge the burden of proof on an insured. The insurers did not dispute that, in principle, an

> undercounting ratio could be used to attempt to ascertain the likely number of actual cases of COVID-19, but they submitted that it could only be used if it could be shown to produce a reliable (not merely reasonable) estimate. Their caveat was that it would depend on the methodology and the underlying data, but those matters could not be tested in the present case."

The UK Government provides time-series data[48] updated on an ongoing basis as to the regional R value, i.e. the rate at which COVID-19 is spreading in any particular area. An excerpt from that data shows the R value from May 2020 in the UK as a whole and in a number of regions:

Date	**UK**		**England**		**East of England**		**London**	
	Lower bound	Upper bound	Lower bound	Upper bound	Lower bound	Upper bound	Lower bound	Upper bound
29-May-20	0.7	0.9	0.7	0.9	.	.	.	.
05-Jun-20	0.7	0.9	0.7	1.0	.	.	.	.
12-Jun-20	0.7	0.9	0.8	1.0	0.7	0.9	0.8	1.0
19-Jun-20	0.7	0.9	0.7	0.9	0.7	0.9	0.7	1.0
26-Jun-20	0.7	0.9	0.7	0.9	0.7	0.9	0.6	0.9
03-Jul-20	0.7	0.9	0.8	0.9	0.7	0.9	0.8	1.1
10-Jul-20	0.7	0.9	0.8	1.0	0.7	1.0	0.7	1.0
17-Jul-20	0.7	0.9	0.8	1.0	0.8	1.0	0.8	1.1
24-Jul-20	0.7	0.9	0.8	1.0	0.8	1.0	0.8	1.0
31-Jul-20	0.8	0.9	0.8	1.0	0.7	1.0	0.8	1.0
07-Aug-20	0.8	1.0	0.8	1.0	0.7	0.9	0.8	1.1
14-Aug-20	0.8	1.0	0.8	1.0	0.8	1.0	0.8	1.0
21-Aug-20	0.9	1.1	0.9	1.0	0.8	1.0	0.9	1.1

48 https://www.gov.uk/guidance/the-r-value-and-growth-rate

28-Aug-20	0.9	1.1	0.9	1.1	0.8	1.0	0.9	1.1
04-Sep-20*	0.9	1.1	0.9	1.0	0.8	1.0	0.9	1.1
11-Sep-20	1.0	1.2	1.0	1.2	0.9	1.2	1.1	1.3
18-Sep-20	1.1	1.4	1.2	1.4	1.0	1.3	1.1	1.4
25-Sep-20	1.2	1.5	1.2	1.5	1.1	1.3	1.2	1.5
02-Oct-20	1.3	1.6	1.2	1.6	1.0	1.3	1.2	1.6
09-Oct-20	1.2	1.5	1.2	1.5	1.3	1.6	1.2	1.4
16-Oct-20	1.3	1.5	1.2	1.4	1.3	1.5	1.1	1.4
23-Oct-20	1.2	1.4	1.2	1.4	1.2	1.4	1.1	1.3
30-Oct-20	1.1	1.3	1.1	1.3	1.2	1.4	1.1	1.3

The above R values can be used to estimate an undercounting ratio to apply to the available data. The basic point is that if the value is greater than 1, then on average each person is likely to be infecting more than one other person and the epidemic can be described as "growing". If the R value is substantially higher than 1, then the more so, such that it might be inferred that the likely number of actual cases exceeds the number of reported cases.

The calculation can be fairly complex and claimants will likely need to seek expert evidence to arrive at robust methodologies for undercounting ratios. The FCA's Covid-19 Calculator seeks to provide an accessible means of estimating cases, using both the data as to reported cases and the Imperial College Estimated Cases data, which the FCA has defended as reliable in its final guidance on proving the presence of Covid-19[49].

---

49 https://www.fca.org.uk/publication/finalised-guidance/final-guidance-bi-insurance-test-case-proving-presence-covid-19.pdf (see Chapter 8).

Obtaining Evidence

Expert actuarial evidence is likely to be necessary to give the court a percentage likelihood based on the facts of the case. Although a claimant could in theory simply rely on internet searches and downloaded data from the ONS and NHS which is freely available, the statistical methodology in proving the likelihood of COVID-19 at certain premises needs to be robust enough to stand up to scrutiny. It is unlikely that a judge at trial would be content to apply some methodology to the data themselves. An actuary would need to be able to provide an answer to the question: "What is the probability, in percentage terms, of a person infected with COVID-19 being on the premises during [x] week(s) prior to [y] lockdown?".

Practically useful evidence would probably also include the following details, along with supporting documentary evidence if available, not only prior to the first lockdown, but also prior to subsequent lockdowns (which, depending on the policy wording could at least arguably by different events):-

(a) how many staff, customers or others entered the premises each day/week;

(b) whether any of those people visibly had, or had reported symptoms, such as a cough, high temperature, a loss of taste or smell, or anything which could suggest COVID-19;

(c) whether anyone who had entered the premises had tested positive for COVID-19;

(d) whether there is anything local to the premises, such as a hospital, a testing centre, a care-home, a walk-in centre, or anything else which may increase the risk of staff or customers in the surrounding area, who may enter the premises with COVID-19;

(e) what the NHS and ONS data available for the area suggest the likely infection-rate is.

A useful resource on proving manifestation is now available in the form of the FCA's final guidance of 3rd March 2021, available at https://www.fca.org.uk/publication/finalised-guidance/final-guidance-bi-insurance-test-case-proving-presence-covid-19.pdf

The FCA also provides a tool to assist in calculating the probability of COVID-19 having been present within a geographical area centred on a post-code. The FCA's calculator includes data from Imperial College starting around the time of the first lockdown. It can be found at https://covidcalculator.fca.org.uk/

CHAPTER NINE

DENIAL OF ACCESS CLAUSES

The Supreme Court in FCA 2[50] gave examples of what are either referred to as "denial of access clauses" or "hybrid clauses". The most straight-forward type of denial of access clause was that used in the Arch policy, as in the form below:

> "loss ... resulting from ... Prevention of access to the Premises due to the actions or advice of a government or local authority due to an emergency which is likely to endanger life or property"

The above wording contains no reference to COVID-19 specifically, although the use of the phrase "emergency which is likely to endanger life or property" was taken to apply to the circumstances of the pandemic, as accepted by Arch in the FCA 1 case[51].

The two examples of hybrid clauses given in FCA 2 were RSA1:

> "loss as a result of closure or restrictions placed on the Premises as a result of a notifiable human disease manifesting itself at the Premises or within a radius of 25 miles of the Premises"

and Hiscox 1-4:

---

50 Para. 96.

51 Para. 310.

> "losses resulting solely and directly from an interruption to your activities caused by your inability to use the insured premises due to restrictions imposed by a public authority during the period of insurance following an occurrence of any human infectious or human contagious disease, an outbreak of which must be notified to the local authority"

The main differences between such hybrid clauses and straightforward denial of access clauses is the reference either to a notifiable disease manifesting within a defined policy area, or restrictions imposed by a public authority following an occurrence of a notifiable disease. Those two alternative wordings have important effects: the "force of law point", the interpretation of what "closure" of the premises, or "inability to use" the premises means, and more generally on the issue of causation.

<u>The Force of Law Point</u>

Business interruption for the purposes of hybrid clauses has to be due to "restrictions" imposed and the court in FCA 2 held that "restrictions" could be either as a result of legal restrictions as well as guidance issued in sufficiently mandatory terms.

In FCA 1, the court discussed the point from paragraph 266 onwards in relation to the Hiscox 1-4 clauses and decided that the term "restrictions imposed" did not include anything less than something which had the force of law, i.e. the restrictions promulgated by statutory instrument:

> 266. We begin with the issue of what is meant by "restrictions imposed" by a public authority. The issue has to be addressed by considering the words used and the context in which they are used. In our view, what these words mean is something which is mandatory, and they do not include something which is less than mandatory. This is the natural meaning of "imposed". Furthermore, these words are used in the context of a resulting inability on the part of the insured to use its own premises. That reinforces

> the conclusion that what is being referred to is something that has the force of law....
>
> 267. What this means for present purposes is that the only relevant matters which constituted "restrictions imposed" are those which were promulgated by statutory instrument, and in particular Regulation 2 of the 21 March Regulations and Regulations 4 and 5 of the 26 March Regulations. Guidance, exhortation and advice given by the Government, including by the Prime Minister, including as to social distancing, do not count as "restrictions imposed" by a public authority. Nor would cases in which people decided not to visit premises, notwithstanding that they were legally permitted to do so, be caused by any "restrictions imposed".

On appeal by the FCA and the Hiscox Interveners the Supreme Court took a different view. The His cox Interveners and FCA made the point that policies are meant to be readily understandable by unsophisticated small businesses and that and reasonable person listening to the Prime Minister's announcements would not consider that they were being given a choice as to whether or not to comply with the directions being given.

The Supreme Court expressed the view that it is not uncommon for a mandatory instruction to be given by a public authority in anticipation of legally binding measures to follow shortly afterwards and, although it agreed with the court below that ordinarily the imposition of restrictions would be understood as meaning restrictions imposed pursuant to statutory or other legal powers, that would not always be the case. An example of that was given at paragraph 118 of the judgment:

> 118. For example, a public health officer who discovers vermin on inspection of a restaurant may issue an immediate instruction to close the restaurant, although the legal order to do so may only follow later. All concerned would expect such an instruction to be complied with

> forthwith, regardless of legalities, and would regard the "restriction" as being "imposed" there and then.

Specifically, in relation to the Prime Minister's guidance, the court in FCA 2 took the view that it was in sufficiently clear and mandatory terms as to amount to a "restriction imposed":

> 120. Whilst one would expect "restrictions imposed" generally to have the force of law or to carry the imminent threat of legal compulsion, we do not accept that the phrase is limited in its meaning to an exercise or threatened exercise of legal powers, as this case illustrates. When the Prime Minister in his statement of 20 March 2020 instructed named businesses to close "tonight", that was a clear, mandatory instruction given on behalf of the UK Government. It was an instruction which both the named businesses and the public would reasonably understand had to be complied with without inquiring into the legal basis or anticipated legal basis for the instruction. We consider that such an instruction is capable of being a "restriction imposed", regardless of whether it was legally capable of being enforced.

The nature of "restriction"

An issue arose in relation to the Hiscox 1-4 policies as to whether "restrictions" had to be directed towards the business itself, or whether more general restrictions could suffice for the purposes of business interruption cover. At paragraph 125 the court in FCA 2 explained the argument by Hiscox that restrictions which prevented people from leaving their homes without reasonable excuse could amount to restrictions on businesses. In FCA 1, the court rejected Hiscox's argument (see paragraph 269 in FCA 2), giving the hypothetical example of a police cordon imposed following a murder unconnected with the business which prevented access to a shop:

> "… such a police cordon would constitute a 'restriction imposed' in that it would be unlawful to cross it without

> proper excuse. Its effect would be to keep the public away, but it would not be directed either to the insured or to the insured's use of the premises."

The Supreme Court took the view that Hiscox's arguments against that decision ought not to succeed. The Supreme Court took the view that the reference to "restrictions imposed" within the policy wording were "general and unqualified" and that whilst most restrictions would be directed at the insured premises or the use of insured premises they were not required to be so directed by the wording of the policies[52]:

> ... The court's police cordon example is relevant as an illustration of an inability to use the premises resulting not from a restriction directed at the premises or their use by the policyholder, but from a restriction which keeps the public out. Having full regard to context, we do not consider that the general words used should be read down in the way that Hiscox contends.

Inability to use

A successful appeal by the FCA and Hiscox Action Group against the High Court decision related to the definition of "inability to use". The court at first instance had taken the view[53] that those words meant a complete inability to use premises, save for use that is *de minimis.*

> ... In our view this [phrase 'inability to use'] plainly does not embrace any and every impairment of normal use. 'Unable to use' means something significantly different from 'hindered in using' or similar ...

52 See para. 128 of FCA 2.

53 See para. 268 in FCA 1.

In a somewhat more nuanced decision, the Supreme Court accepted that the issue was binary- i.e. that the court below was right to hold that an *inability* to use has to be established, as opposed to an impairment or hindrance in use, but accepted, on the other hand, the arguments of the FCA and HAG that it would be uncommercial to require that every part of the premises, for every purposes was unable to be used. The Supreme Court's view was that where the operations of the business or the premises could be regarded as being divided into discrete parts, a complete inability to use some such part of the premises or of the business would fall within the scope of cover.

The Supreme Court gave some examples[54] where an inability to use parts of the business or premises might still fall within the scope of cover:-

1. A bookshop required to close with the loss of all of its walk-in customer business, representing 80% of its income, but still able to process telephone orders representing 20% of its income.

2. A department store which had to close all parts of the store except its pharmacy.

3. A golf course which is allowed to remain open for playing golf, but required to close its clubhouse for serving food and drinks, or hosting functions.

Similarly, as indicated above, the Supreme Court applied similar principles to prevention of access to discrete parts of premises:

> 151. In our view, for essentially the same reasons as given in relation to Hiscox 1- 4, the Arch wording may, depending on the facts, cover prevention of access to a discrete part of the premises and/or for the purpose of carrying on a discrete part of the policyholder's business

54 See para. 138 onwards in FCA 2.

> activities. We agree with Arch that prevention means stopping something from happening or making an intended act impossible and is different from mere hindrance. In both the situations contemplated, however, access to a discrete part of the premises or access to the premises for a discrete purpose will have been completely stopped from happening.

<u>Causation in "at the Premises" cases</u>

Also of relevance to some Disease Clauses as well as Hybrid Clauses is an argument soon to be decided by the High Court that there is a distinction in the interpretation to be adopted between manifestation of disease within a specified policy area, such as within a defined radius of the premises and cases where the clause requires manifestation to be "at the premises".

On one view, the approach on causation adopted by the Supreme Court in radius cases ought to apply to cases of manifestation at the premises. The argument is that in principle there ought not to be a distinction between a policy area specified to be a radius of 10 miles of the premises, 1 mile of the premises, 0.5 miles of the premises, or the curtilage of the premises itself. The rationale almost explains itself: that the policy area is solely a matter of distance within which a policy wording specified that disease must be manifested, and that the evidential burden becomes more easy or more difficult to discharge naturally depending on the size of the defined policy area.

The argument put forward by insurers, however, is that where the policy requires manifestation at the premises, the parties reasonably intended cover to extend to the sorts of claims where the disease is localised or directly related to the premises, as opposed to more general outbreaks which happen to also have manifested at the premises. An example of such circumstances is the familiar reference within disease clauses to outbreaks of legionella, food-poisoning, or other defects in sanitary arrangements at the premises, which all arise of circumstances specific to the premises covered by the policy, rather than national outbreaks of disease.

Some insurers have relied on the FCA's written submissions before the Supreme Court in order to explain the point:

> 194. Each clause must be construed in its particular context, but at least where, as here, these clauses exist alongside radius clauses, <u>the nature of the cover provided by these 'at the premises' clauses is different because the contemplated interruption (and authority action) caused by a disease occurring at the premises will be different to interruption (and authority action) caused by a disease occurring away from the premises.</u> In the former case, the premises is likely the source of the disease (as is explicitly required in relation to a food or drink part of such clauses), and the risk is that it continues to produce that disease or illness— as in the case of Legionnaire's disease or food poisoning, and/or that the disease may get out of the premises and, in so doing, spread to others. The clause envisages measures directed specifically at the premises to stop that repetition or spread; measures that would not be taken on a national or wide area basis. The fortuity is therefore, as a matter of construction, contemplating and limited to the at-the-premises aspect of any disease, not a wider outbreak.
>
> 195. <u>The radius clause is different; it recognises instead that the insured could get caught up in measures which are not directed at or specific to the policyholder at all</u>, but which are taken to suppress an outbreak of a notifiable disease that is present anywhere within that radius, including for public health reasons. The reason the business is interrupted is usually (where any case within 25 miles triggers the clause) not because of a concern that the premises is a source of infection, nor that the fabric of the premises may itself become infected. The primary reasons are more likely that the disease may be spread by people being in close proximity to each other (which the authority aims to prevent), as a result of travelling to or from of visiting or working at business premises (either generally or of within

categories into which the insured's business falls); and/or that an outbreak will suppress the insured's own trade, such as by reduced footfall. In those circumstances, 'within a radius of 25 miles of the premises' is adjectival and the intention is to cover outbreaks inside and outside the radius, whereas 'at the premises' limits the fortuity requiring a link between the occurrence at the premises and the interruption.

CHAPTER TEN

THE MEASURE OF LOSS

Losses in business interruption cases are nearly always defined in relatively specific terms by the policy and the schedule.

Many, if not most policies define losses for interruption to business on the basis of an assessment of gross profits during the period of loss in comparison to gross profits during the preceding year, subject to reasonable adjustments and business trends, and along with other items of loss such as the increased cost of working, and various fees.

Losses are normally specified to only be payable during a limited period known as the indemnity period, often 12 or 24 months and subject to indemnity limits being the maximum sum claimable.

The Limit of Indemnity

Policies usually specify the limit of indemnity applicable to claims for business interruption in a table in the policy schedule. Many businesses assume that that is the applicable limit to business interruption claims arising from the pandemic, and it may be, but more often individual policy clauses specify an inner limit of indemnity of a lesser sum.

By way of example, a policy schedule might state as follows:

Commercial Combined Policy – SECTION 2 (Business Interruption)		
Basis A	Loss of gross profits	£2,000,000.00
	Specified additional increased cost of working	£100,000.00
	Maximum Indemnity Period	12 months
Basis B	Loss of gross revenue	Not insured
	Increased cost of working	Not Insured
	Maximum Indemnity Period	12 months
Basis C	Loss of gross rental income	£500,000.00
	Increased cost of working	£100,000.00
	Maximum Indemnity Period	12 months

Although the figure of £2,000,000 in the above example might be taken to apply to all causes of business interruption, care should be taken as to whether the sum is stated to apply to business interruption losses arising from material damage only (as it is in many policies) and even then, the relevant disease clause within the policy wording itself, as below, may impose an inner limit of indemnity (in this example £100,000):

> **14. Murder suicide or disease**
>
> The Insurer will indemnify the Insured in respect of loss ... as a result of
>
> a) the occurrence of any of the following specified human infectious or human contagious diseases:
>
> > i. Acute Encephalitis
> >
> > ii. Acute Poliomyelitis
> >
> > iii. Anthrax
> >
> > ...

b) murder or suicide at the Premises

c) injury or illness sustained by any person arising from ...

d) The discovery of vermin or pests in the Building(s) ...

e) the closing of the whole or part of the premises by order of the public authority...

i. This cover will only apply for the period starting with the occurrence of the loss and ending after 12 weeks during which time the results of the Business are affected

ii. The Insurer will not cover any costs incurred in the cleaning repair replacement recall or checking of the property insured

<u>iii. The maximum the Insurer will pay for any one claim is £100,000</u>

Claims may therefore be substantially more limited in scope that appears at first sight. There are arguments, however, which may be made as to whether that inner limit of indemnity applies only to one particular claim for business interruption. There may be merit in such arguments depending on whether the interruption occurs at separate premises in the same business, or in sufficiently disconnected periods of time such that the loss could be said to arise as a separate claim. Nevertheless, some policies contain very clear aggregation clauses which impose the same inner limits of indemnity to *all claims* within a particular indemnity period.

<u>The Indemnity Period</u>

The period of indemnity is often specified in the schedule and policy wording generally, and on a "per-clause" basis in a similar way to how the limits of indemnity are specified.

The period, however, as can be seen in the above example, has relevance in more than one way. The period is normally defined in the policy as that period within which insurable loss will be paid under its terms. For example, if loss is caused at a particular time during the policy, where there is an indemnity period of 12 months, then the insured would be able to claim for losses continuing from that time, for a period of 12 months, and that period might extend past the period of the policy. Sometimes, however, the indemnity period is defined not only with respect to how long the losses persist, but is also used within some clauses to define when during the period of the policy claims may be brought.

Trends Clauses

In FCA 2, the court said:

> "251. All the sample policy wordings considered in these proceedings contain clauses of a kind generally known as trends clauses. Such clauses are part of the standard method used in insurance policies that provide business interruption cover for quantifying the policyholder's financial loss. All of the insurers who appeal against the decision of the court below do so on the issue of how the trends clauses apply in the circumstances of the present case. It is the insurers' contention that the trends clauses have the effect that they are not liable to indemnify policyholders for losses which would have arisen regardless of the operation of the insured perils by reason of the wider consequences of the COVID-19 pandemic."

An example of a trends clause applying to business interruption cover based on a loss in annual gross revenue is as follows:

> **Annual Gross Revenue Basis**
>
> The Gross Revenue during the twelve months immediately before the date of the damage to which such adjustment to be made as may be necessary to provide for the trend of the

Business and for variations in or special circumstances affecting the Business either before or after the damage or which would have affected the Business had the damage not occurred so that the figures thus adjusted shall represent as nearly as may be reasonably practicable the results which but for the damage would have been obtained during the Period after the damage.

There will no doubt be specific factors in different cases which could be relied on to support either side in their contentions that revenue might have been higher or lower in the year of the loss, compared with the previous year. A particular business might have been doing well enough to have expected a higher revenue in the year of the loss than in the previous year, when, for example they may have had fewer staff, or smaller premises. Equally, something specific during the year preceding the loss might have artificially depressed turnover, such as a strike.

The Supreme Court gave specific guidance in paragraphs 259 to 264 about how to interpret trends clauses in the context of the pandemic:-

1. Trends clauses are a part of the machinery in the policy for quantifying loss, but do not address or seek to delineate the scope of cover, which is the function of the insuring clauses within the policy.

2. Trends clauses ought to be interpreted consistently with the insuring clauses in the policy if possible.

3. Such consistent construction means that they should not be construed to take away the cover provided by the insuring clauses, so as to amount, effectively, to a form of exclusion clause, rather than a clause quantifying loss.

In FCA 1, the court had held that:-

1. In the case of disease clauses, the relevant counter-factual for the purposes of making adjustments under trends clauses was the

pandemic not occurring (i.e. revenue earned "but for" the pandemic occurring).

2. In the case of prevention of access and hybrid clauses, the approach was to ascertain what the results of the business would have been if none of the insured perils had occurred, i.e., that there had been (i) no emergency likely to endanger life; (ii) no consequent public authority action; and (iii) no consequent prevention of access to the premises.

That interpretation had to be rejected by the Supreme Court, because it had rejected the "but for" test for causation in disease clauses, and, as regards prevention of access and hybrid clauses, it had found that the composite insured peril involved a number of interconnected elements in causal sequence.

The Supreme Court's view[55] was that, absent clear wording, one should recognise that the aim of such trends clauses is to arrive at the revenue that would have been achieved but for the insured peril and circumstances arising out of the same underlying or originating cause, such that the business trends referred to within the trends clauses should generally be construed as meaning trends or circumstances unrelated to the insured peril.

To demonstrate its interpretation, the Supreme Court used the example[56] of a fashion-wear business which runs a shop and also sells via a website. The business is forced to close part of its business, the shop, by the effect of reg. 5(1) of the 26th March Regulations, but continues to trade via its website. The court took the view that in those circumstances, the business would only be covered for interruption to its shop's sales, but not to its website's sales, even if those were perhaps lower during the course of the pandemic. Applying the above interpretation of trends clauses in making adjustments, the business

---

55 Para. 268 in FCA 2.

56 Para. 281 in FCA 2.

would have to compare only its shop's turnover to the turnover from the shop during the previous year (the standard turnover). In that way, one ignores from the adjustment the other consequences of the pandemic, i.e. in this case, the reduction to the sales from the website, which arose from the same underlying circumstances of the pandemic, but which itself fell outside the scope of the insuring clauses:

> "286. The result will be that the amount recoverable by the policyholder will not be reduced if, had the shop not been compelled to close, its turnover would have been lower in any event as a result of other consequences of the pandemic. Nor will it be increased if, had the shop been allowed to remain open in circumstances where all its competitors were forced to close, its turnover would have been higher. At the same time the policyholder will not be able to recover any loss caused by a fall in website orders as such loss is not covered."

<u>Double Insurance</u>

Issues often arise between the insurer and insured where more than one policy of insurance exists, providing overlapping insurance and a decision must be taken as to which policy responds and to what extent. Predictably, both policies may provide for such circumstances.

An example (1) is as follows:

> "**Other insurances**
>
> If any claim covered under this policy is also covered by another policy, or would have been covered if this policy did not exist, **we** will only pay **our** share of the claim even if the other insurer refuses the claim."

The "other" policy states (2):

> **"Other Insurance**
>
> If the insurance provided by these sections is also covered by another policy (or would but for the existence of these sections) **We** will only indemnify **You** in respect of any excess beyond the amount which would be payable under such other insurance had these sections not been effected."

There are various legal criteria in relation to whether double insurance exists, such as, for example, whether the insured obtained the insurance or whether it was obtained by someone else on their behalf in a variety of circumstances, whether the interest being insured is the same interest, as opposed to different interests in the same loss, and a number of other matters beyond the scope of this book. Assuming that double insurance exists, the question to consider in the case of the above example is what takes place when a rateable proportion clause (1) appears to conflict with an excess clause (2).

Colinvaux's Law of Insurance, 12th Ed. Defines rateable proportion clauses at 12-161 as follows:

> "**Rateable proportion" clauses.** Rateable proportion clauses differ in their wording, but the broad intention of such clauses is to limit the insurer's liability to the assured to its share of the loss if, at the time of the loss, any other insurance covering the same risk is in effect. The main consequence of such a clause so far as the assured is concerned is to limit his right to proceed against the various insurers in the order of his choice, although his ultimate ability to claim an indemnity is not affected: in the result, then, the contribution takes place at the stage at which the assured has made a claim rather than at the later stage at which one or more insurers have met the loss in full and seek to proceed against other insurers for contribution."

The two important cases regarding the potential for tension between rateable proportion clauses and excess clauses are *State Fire Insurance v Liverpool & London Globe Insurance*[57] (a New Zealand decision) and *National Farmers Union Mutual Insurance Society Ltd v HSBC Insurance (UK) Ltd.*[58]

The *State Fire Insurance* case established the principle that excess clauses override rateable proportion clauses. For example, if Policy A contains an excess clause and Policy B contains a rateable proportion clause, Policy A will not cover the loss *by reason of* Policy B and the rateable proportion clause in Policy B cannot apply because there is no other available cover (i.e. Policy A has not been engaged).

In *State Fire Insurance*, Policy A contained an excess clause *and* a rateable proportion clause, and Policy B contained a rateable proportion clause *only*. The court ruled that the rateable proportion clause was to be subordinated to the excess clause, so that Policy A could not respond until Policy B's cover had been exhausted, and Policy B had to pay out the whole loss because, until it did, Policy A did not attach.

In *NFU Mutual*[59], the sellers of a building were insured against damage to it, and their policy also provided cover for the buyers under the following clause:

> "We will not pay any claim if any loss, damage or liability covered under **this** insurance is also covered wholly or in part under any **other** insurance except in respect of any excess beyond the amount which would have been covered under such **other** insurance had **this** insurance not been effected."

The buyers were also insured under a policy that said:

---

57 [1952] N.Z.L.R. 5.

58 [2010] EWHC 773 (Comm); [2010] 1 C.L.C. 557.

59 See summary in *Colinvaux* at 12-164

> "[i]f when you claim there is other insurance covering the same accident, illness, damage or liability, we will only pay our share"

After the property was damaged by fire between the exchange of contracts and completion of the conveyance, the buyers paid the full contract price and claimed an indemnity from their insurers. Their insurers then claimed a contribution from the sellers' insurance on the basis that the sellers' policy provided cover for the buyers and therefore created double insurance.

Gavin Kealey QC in *NFU Mutual* dismissed the claim on the basis of there being no double insurance, but expressed the view (contrary to Tucker J, in the case of *Austin*) that excess clauses override rateable proportion clauses.

In *Austin*, one insurer had a rateable proportion clause and an escape clause (completely avoiding an indemnity in the event that there existed other insurance) and the *other* insurer had an escape clause and an excess clause. Kealey QC took the view, perhaps uncontroversially, that the escape clauses cancelled each other out (if they didn't then nobody would be liable), leaving an excess clause conflicting with a rateable proportion clause. He doubted (compellingly in my view) the reasoning of Tucker J that there should simply be a 50/50 rating between the two insurers.

A similar decision was reached in *Chui Man Kwan v Bank of China Group Insurance Co Ltd.*[60] (a Hong Kong case) based on the following clause:

> "If at the time of any claim under this policy there is any other insurance indemnifying any person or insured or insureds who are entitled to be indemnified under this policy, this policy is not to be called upon in contribution

60 [2008] H.K.E.C. 1190.

> and, subject to the policy limits of indemnity, is only to pay any amount if and so far as not recoverable under such other insurance."

The court ruled that the excess clause only responded when the other insurer's indemnity had been exhausted and in that case the policy with the rateable proportion clause covered the entire loss, such that the policy with the excess clause did not respond at all.

The bulk of the authority on the point about such conflicts seems to weigh on the side of rateable proportion clauses being overridden by excess clauses. Each policy will depend on a construction of its wording, based on the reasonably ascertainable intentions of the parties to each contract and there may be circumstances where wording additional to that set out above might be taken to qualify the excess clause.

Business interruption policies frequently contain such clauses, and are important to consider. They may be of general application within the policy or may be applied to certain sections only.

CHAPTER ELEVEN

INSURANCE CLAIMS

Notification of Claims

Policies make provision for claims notification with varying degrees of formality. Although some make little or no such provision, others set out procedures which ought, as a matter of contract, to be complied with. An example from a Commercial Combined policy provides:

> "**8 Claims notification and procedures**
>
> In the event of any incident which may give rise to a claim, the *Insured* must notify the
>
> *Insurers* or the *Insurance Broker* as soon as practicable giving full details of what has happened.
>
> If the *Insured* fails to notify the *Insurers* or the *Insurance Broker* within
>
> > **i** 7 (seven) days in the case of *Damage* caused by riot, civil commotion, strikers, locked out workers or persons taking part in labour disturbances or malicious persons;
> >
> > **ii** 30 (thirty) days of the expiry of the *Indemnity Period* in respect of a claim under Insured Section 2 of *Your Policy*;
> >
> > **iii** 30 (thirty) days working days of any allegation or claim which could rise to a claim under Insured Sections 7, 8 or 9…"

Other policies make specific provision for notification to be made in writing, to specific addresses, and it is of course important to check those matters as soon as possible when considering whether to bring a claim.

Clauses making such stipulations are usually regarded as "Non-core terms" for the purposes of regulatory control over policies and, especially in the circumstances of the pandemic and the delays resulting from the FCA litigation, regulatory pressure on insurers not to deny cover solely on the basis of late notification may be sufficient for the purposes of many policy-holders. It may, for example, for the FCA's purposes amount to unfair conduct for such claims to be denied in certain circumstances.

There are a number of cases which dealt with "immediate notice" clauses, however, there is no fixed definition of the term, which has been said to mean "with all reasonable speed considering the circumstances of the case"[61].

Where fixed notice periods are provided in the policy, the insured is required to comply with them strictly[62], however, arguments have arisen as to when differing types of loss sufficiently manifest themselves to insureds and it may be that arguments develop as to when interruption to business resulting from the pandemic meet that threshold.

---

61 See Colinvaux's Law of Insurance, 12th Ed. at 10-013, citing Re Coleman's Depositories [1907] 2 K.B. 798; Aspen Insurance UK Ltd v Pectel Ltd. [2009] Lloyd's Rep. I.R. 440; AXA Insurance UK Plc v Thermonex Ltd. [2012] EWHC B10 (Mercantile Court), where the assured became aware of damage at the end of 2003 but did not notify the insurers until November 2005; Milton Keynes BC v Nulty [2012] Lloyd's Rep. I.R. 453: where there was an 18-month gap between the assured becoming aware of a liability for fire damage and notice of the fire being given.

62 See *Colinvaux* at 10-015

Arbitration Clauses

Policies frequently make provision for the parties to arbitrate, which will, save in the case of agreement, bind the parties.

Where arbitration clauses exist, they are usually in two forms: those providing for arbitration of any issue arising between the parties, including the issue of whether there is cover in principle, and those providing for arbitration solely on the issue of quantum. For example:

> "**Governing law**. Unless some other law is agreed in writing, this policy will be governed by the laws of England.
>
> **Arbitration**. Any dispute arising out of or relating to this insurance, including over its construction, application and validity, will be referred to a single arbitrator in accordance with the Arbitration Act then in force."
>
> and
>
> "**Arbitration.** If any difference shall arise as to the amount to be paid under this Certificate (liability being otherwise admitted) such difference shall be referred to an arbitrator to be appointed by the parties in accordance with the Statutory provisions in that behalf for the time being in force. Where any difference is by this condition to be referred to arbitration the making of an award shall be a condition precedent of any right of action against the Underwriters"

The effect of such clauses is that, bar a dispute as to the arbitrability of the dispute, for example, on the basis of a rule of law requiring to be decided, the parties will be required to comply with the provisions of the Arbitration Act 1996, as amended, and appoint an arbitrator in accordance with the provisions agreed in the policy (which, as long as they comply with the Act, may be as prescriptive or as vague as the parties have agreed in the policy).

Although arbitration generally is a subject beyond the scope of this book, a few points are worth making in relation to business interruption cases.

The Arbitration Act 1996

Section 1 of the Act sets out the general principles to be adopted in construction of Pt I of that act:

> "(a) the object of arbitration is to obtain the fair resolution of disputes by an impartial tribunal without unnecessary delay or expense;
>
> (b) the parties should be free to agree how their disputes are resolved, subject only to such safeguards as are necessary in the public interest;
>
> (c) in matters governed by [Pt I] the court should not intervene except as provided in this Part"

The Act in general provides flexibility in the manner in which arbitrations are conducted and its provisions place significant emphasis on the parties being entitled to agree most matters relating to the arbitral tribunal, its composition, what it will decide and how it works.

Form of Agreement

There is no particular prescribed form[63] for a valid agreement to arbitrate, and it is likely that the above examples from insurance policies will be sufficient to amount to a valid agreement to arbitrate.

---

63 See, for example, *Transamerican Ocean Contractors Inc v Transchemical Rotterdam* BV [1978] 1 Lloyd's Rep. 238, where an agreement provided simply "...& arbitration in London".

Legal Proceedings

In the event that one party brings proceedings in court under a policy, where there is a valid arbitration agreement, that amounts to no defence to the claim, but the other party may apply to stay[64] the proceedings. Further, damages may be awarded against the party bringing the proceedings in breach of the arbitration agreement.

Commencement of Arbitral Proceedings

If the parties have not already agreed (per s.14(1)) when arbitral proceedings are regarded as having commenced, subsections 14(3) to (5) of the Act provide as follows:

> "(3) Where the arbitrator is named or designated in the arbitration agreement, arbitral proceedings are commenced in respect of a matter when one party serves on the other party or parties a notice in writing requiring him or them to submit that matter to the person so named or designated.
>
> (4) Where the arbitrator or arbitrators are to be appointed by the parties, arbitral proceedings are commenced in respect of a matter when one party serves on the other party or parties notice in writing requiring him or them to appoint an arbitrator or to agree to the appointment of an arbitrator in respect of that matter.
>
> (5) Where the arbitrator or arbitrators are to be appointed by a person other than a party to the proceedings, arbitral proceedings are commenced in respect of a matter when one party gives notice in writing to that person requesting him to make the appointment in respect of that matter."

---

64 See *Chitty on Contracts,* 33rd Ed. at 32-051

The Arbitral Tribunal[65]

The parties are free to agree the composition of the tribunal including the number of arbitrators to form the tribunal and whether there is to be a chairman or umpire. Unless otherwise agreed by the parties, an agreement that the number of arbitrators shall be two or any other even number shall be understood as requiring the appointment of an additional arbitrator as chairman of the tribunal. If there is no agreement as to the number of arbitrators, the tribunal shall consist of a sole arbitrator.

Court Claims

The usual method of bringing proceedings such as these to court is by issuing a Part 7 Claim Form in the claimant's local Business and Property Court, whether that is in the County Court list or in the High Court, based on the usual decision as to value and complexity, followed by Particulars of Claim, similar to those in the Appendix below. The defendant insurer will have an opportunity to file a defence and the matter will in all likelihood be listed for a Costs and Case Management Conference at which the parties will budget their costs, and receive directions to timetable the claim towards trial.

There are, however, two qualifications to that approach. Firstly, the claim might be decided earlier than at trial, i.e. at a Summary Judgment hearing under Part 24 of the Civil Procedure Rules 1998 (dealt with in more detail below). Secondly, in what is likely to be a very limited number of cases, there may be scope for use of the Financial Markets Test Case Scheme (FMTCS), now contained in Practice Direction 63AA.

65 See s.15 of the Arbitration Act 1996.

The FMTCS

The key features of the FMTCS are that it can only be used by mutual agreement, and that the general rule is that there will be no order for costs:

> "**Financial Markets Test Case Scheme**
>
> **6.1** The Financial Markets Test Case Scheme applies to a claim started in the Financial List which is a Financial List claim and which raises issues of general importance in relation to which immediately relevant authoritative English law guidance is needed ("a qualifying claim").
>
> **6.2** In such cases the Financial Markets Test Case Scheme enables the qualifying claim to be determined without the need for a present cause of action between the parties to the proceedings.
>
> **Proceedings in the Financial Markets Test Case Scheme**
>
> **6.3** Where there is a qualifying claim a person who is or was actively in business in the relevant market may, by mutual agreement, issue proceedings against another person who is or was actively in business in the relevant market provided that other person has opposing interests as to how the law of England and Wales issue(s) raised by the qualifying claim should be resolved.
>
> **6.4** The claim form must indicate clearly that the claim is brought pursuant to the Financial List, Financial Markets Test Case Scheme.
>
> **6.5** … (c) the general rule will be that there shall be no order as to costs;
>
> …"

Costs in Normal Proceedings

One of the biggest concerns for businesses struggling with the financial effects of the pandemic is the issue of legal costs in the event that they lose their claim. The usual rule under CPR Part 44 applies, i.e. that the losing party pays the winner's costs of the claim. As a matter of financial regulation, rather than civil procedure, however, the FCA has written to businesses suggesting that in cases which raise points of wider public importance, they would expect that insurers would take a reasonable view on the issue of costs, and it may be that, depending on the circumstances of the case, the FCA takes the view that an insurer seeking substantial legal costs is a matter of concern to them.

Insolvency

Many insurance policies include a clause declining cover in the event that a business becomes insolvent, which is important to check before bringing a claim. An example appears below:

> "**Conditions**
>
> The following conditions apply to this Section in addition to the Policy Conditions at the back of this policy.
>
> We will not cover You under this Section if any Policyholder
>
> > (a) agrees a composition or arrangement with creditors, or
> >
> > (b) agrees a proposal for a voluntary arrangement for a composition of debts or a scheme of arrangement approved in accordance with the Insolvency Act 1986 or any successor act, or
> >
> > (c) has an application made under the Insolvency Act 1986 or any successor act to the court for the appointment of an administrator, or

> (d) has a winding up order made or a resolution for voluntary winding up passed except for the purposes of amalgamation or reconstruction, or has a provisional liquidator, receiver, or receiver and manager of The Business duly appointed, or
>
> (e) has an administrative receiver, as defined in the Insolvency Act 1986 or any successor act, appointed or has possession taken by or on behalf of the holders of any debentures secured by floating charge or of any property comprised in or subject to the floating charge"

Interim Remedies

When insurers dispute liability under a policy, the claim is more likely to be decided at the Summary Judgment stage, which can take months, rather than years. That is because these sorts of disputes often involve points of law upon which the parties fundamentally disagree: "Does SARS include COVID-19?", "Can a Claimant rely on the test of causation in 'at the Premises' cases?" and others.

Those sorts of points of law are capable of being decided by a judge at an early stage in proceedings, without the parties having to go through the usual stages of trial preparation, such as costs budgeting, disclosure, exchanging witness statements, obtaining expert evidence and dealing with interim applications. There is therefore a substantial saving in terms of costs because the court will generally only require the parties' legal pleadings, interim witness statements on each side, more limited disclosure of documents, skeleton arguments and the oral arguments of counsel.

The Summary Judgment procedure is set out in CPR Part 24, the relevant rule being CPR 24.2:

Grounds for summary judgment

> **24.2** The court may give summary judgment against a claimant or defendant on the whole of a claim or on a particular issue if –
>
> (a) it considers that –
>
> (i) that claimant has no real prospect of succeeding on the claim or issue; or
>
> (ii) that defendant has no real prospect of successfully defending the claim or issue; and
>
> (b) there is no other compelling reason why the case or issue should be disposed of at a trial.
>
> (Rule 3.4 makes provision for the court to strike out a statement of case or part of a statement of case if it appears that it discloses no reasonable grounds for bringing or defending a claim)

The Summary Judgment jurisdiction overlaps with the court's jurisdiction to strike out a statement of case (i.e. particulars of claim or a defence) if the court is of the view that the claimant or defendant has "no reasonable grounds for bringing or defending the claim".

The effect of rules 24.2 and 3.4 is that a court may decide the claim on the papers, with arguments from counsel, without hearing witnesses as if it were a trial, and without receiving full disclosure and expert evidence. In cases which turn on a substantial factual dispute between the parties, the procedure will often be unsuitable, but where a point of law is likely to decide whether the case succeeds or fails, the court will be better placed to decide the issue at a Summary Judgment hearing.

In business interruption claims, it is usually the defendant insurer who makes an application for Summary Judgment on form N244 after filing their defence. Parties then exchange witness statements exhibiting the evidence upon which they seek to rely, according to the timetable in Part 24, or the timetable in the Commercial Court Guide and the matter is listed for a hearing, which the parties themselves may or may not decide to attend.

Insurance Act 2015

The most relevant section of the Act is s.13A, which creates an action in damages against the insurer for a failure to pay out within a reasonable time:

> **13A Implied term about payment of claims**
>
> (1) It is an implied term of every contract of insurance that if the insured makes a claim under the contract, the insurer must pay any sums due in respect of the claim within a reasonable time.
>
> (2) A reasonable time includes a reasonable time to investigate and assess the claim.
>
> (3) What is reasonable will depend on all the relevant circumstances, but the following are examples of things which may need to be taken into account—
>
> > (a) the type of insurance,
> >
> > (b) the size and complexity of the claim,
> >
> > (c) compliance with any relevant statutory or regulatory rules or guidance,
> >
> > (d) factors outside the insurer's control.
>
> (4) If the insurer shows that there were reasonable grounds for disputing the claim (whether as to the amount of any sum payable, or as to whether anything at all is payable)—
>
> > (a) the insurer does not breach the term implied by subsection (1) merely by failing to pay the claim (or

the affected part of it) while the dispute is continuing, but

(b) the conduct of the insurer in handling the claim may be a relevant factor in deciding whether that term was breached and, if so, when.

(5) Remedies (for example, damages) available for breach of the term implied by subsection (1) are in addition to and distinct from—

(a) any right to enforce payment of the sums due, and

(b) any right to interest on those sums (whether under the contract, under another enactment, at the court's discretion or otherwise).

The Financial Conduct Authority

The FCA operates a complaints process aimed at consumers and small businesses which is less formal and less costly than court proceedings, handled by the Financial Ombudsman Service[66] (FOS).

The FOS handles complaints in relation to insurance, and provides guidance specific to business interruption insurance complaints arising from the COVID-19 pandemic[67].

The powers of the FOS are set out in Part XVI and Schedule 17 of the Financial Services and Markets Act 2000 and decides complaints based on the rules set out in the FCA DISP Handbook[68].

---

66 https://www.financial-ombudsman.org.uk/who-we-are

67 https://sme.financial-ombudsman.org.uk/complain/complaints-can-help/insurance/business-interruption-insurance

68 https://www.handbook.fca.org.uk/handbook/DISP/

The first step in making a complaint to the FOS is to complain to the insurer. Save in exceptional circumstances, complainants have 6 months from the date of the insurer's final response within which to make a complaint to the FOS, after which time the complaint is time-barred[69]:

> "The Ombudsman cannot consider a complaint if the complainant refers it to the Financial Ombudsman Service:
>
> (1) more than six months after the date on which the respondent sent the complainant its final response, redress determination or summary resolution communication; or
>
> (2) more than:
>
> > (a) six years after the event complained of; or (if later)
> >
> > (b) three years from the date on which the complainant became aware (or ought reasonably to have become aware) that he had cause for complaint;
>
> unless the complainant referred the complaint to the respondent or to the Ombudsman within that period and has a written acknowledgement or some other record of the complaint having been received;
>
> ..."

Further, the FOS has eligibility criteria which complainants must meet, under DISP 2.7[70], which requires that complainants be consumers, micro-enterprises, charities, trustees, small businesses, or otherwise listed in DISP 2.7.

Complaints are considered by the FOS in accordance with DISP 3.6.4:

---

69 See DISP 2.8

70 https://www.handbook.fca.org.uk/handbook/DISP/2/7.html

"In considering what is fair and reasonable in all the circumstances of the case, the Ombudsman will take into account:

(1) relevant:

(a) law and regulations;

(b) regulators' rules, guidance and standards;

(c) codes of practice; and

(2) (where appropriate) what he considers to have been good industry practice at the relevant time."

Although final FOS decisions cannot be appealed, it is a public body and is therefore subject to judicial review. The FOS states in its guidance that small businesses are entitled to withdraw from the complaints process at any time, or reject the FOS's determination and instead pursue the matter in court.

The Handbook provision dealing with final determinations is DISP 3.6.6., which states:

"**The Ombudsman's determination**

When the Ombudsman has determined a complaint:

(1) the Ombudsman will give both parties a signed written statement of the determination, giving the reasons for it;

(2) the statement will require the complainant to notify the Ombudsman, before the date specified in the statement, whether he accepts or rejects the determination;

(3) if the complainant notifies the Ombudsman that he accepts the determination within that time limit, it is final and binding on both parties;

(4) subject to paragraph (4A), if the complainant does not notify the Ombudsman that he accepts the determination within that time limit, the complainant will be treated as having rejected the determination, and neither party will be bound by it;

(4A) the complainant is not to be treated as having rejected the determination under paragraph (4) if all the following conditions are met:

(a) the complainant notifies the Ombudsman after the specified date of the complainant's acceptance of the determination;

(b) the complainant has not previously notified the Ombudsman of the complainant's rejection of the determination;

(c) in the view of the Ombudsman, the failure to comply with the time limit for acceptance was as a result of exceptional circumstances;

(5) the Ombudsman will notify the respondent of the outcome and, if the complainant is treated as having rejected the determination under paragraph (4), the effect of paragraph (4A)."

CHAPTER TWELVE

BROKER CLAIMS

Even if your policy doesn't allow you to claim for business interruption, you may very well have a claim against your insurance broker.

Whilst the impression that you are often given is that insurance brokers work for the insurer, they are professionals, like many others, who are there to provide you with advice and act as your agent and in your interests. It is therefore all the more surprising that brokers have ended up putting businesses off from making claims: or perhaps not so surprising given that they may have not provided advice of a sufficient quality at the outset.

Not only have brokers since January 2005 been required to comply with the applicable rules in the current FSA or FCA Hanbook, which may give rise to certain remedies from the regulator, but brokers also have duties, subject to the terms of their contract and instructions, to:

1. identify the type and scope of cover which the client needs, and advise the client accordingly;

2. take reasonable steps to arrange the insurance cover which the client has instructed him to obtain, and which is suitable for and clearly meets the client's requirements;

3. have regard, in placing the insurance, to the obligations of disclosure owed to the insurer;

4. advise the client as to the scope of cover that has and has not been arranged, if unable to arrange the requested cover;

5. consider and explain to the client what cover has been arranged, once the cover has been placed; and

6. go through the same exercise that was carried out at the inception of the policy, when that existing policy is renewed.

Most of the cases in which a broker has been found liable for breach of duty are ones where the broker has failed to act with due skill and care in the performance of one of the roles set out immediately above.

In *Arbory Group Ltd v West Craven Insurance Services*, for example, a parent company of a number of subsidiaries succeeded in making a claim against an insurance broker after it became apparent that it had been under-insured for business interruption as a result of the broker's negligent advice.

The Claimant in *Arbory* had arranged BII through a broker who had failed to advise properly on the correct method of calculating gross profit. When the Claimant's business was devastated by fire and sufficient insurance cover was unavailable, the court allowed the Claimant to recover the shortfall in payment along with damages for loss of profits.

The judge, at para. 51 of the judgment said:

> "51. I am satisfied, therefore, and hold that the duty of the broker in this case where Business Interruption cover was required was to effect such cover that would enable the business of the Group as a whole to recover to its pre incident level of profitability; that the payment of such sum was, as the broker would appreciate, over and above any sums required to cover damage to building and equipment; that, in the circumstances of this type of cover, it was reasonably foreseeable that failure to effect sufficient cover was liable adversely to affect the profitability of the business so insured, if as a result of the broker's negligence insufficient Business Interruption insurance money was paid to enable the company to recover as it should have so recovered in the event that proper cover had been effected."

Most insurance brokers have professional indemnity insurance to cover such claims against them and, as with other types of court claim, insurance funding for litigation against insurance brokers is often available.

CHAPTER THIRTEEN

LITIGATION FUNDING

Substantial developments in the law relating to litigation funding took place during the pandemic. Although funding based on conditional fee agreements (CFAs) has been relatively uncontroversial recently, the decision in *Zuberi v Lexlaw Limited* [2021] EWCA Civ 16 effectively removed many of the restrictions on this type of litigation funding that had existed since the Damages Based Agreements Regulations 2013 were brought into force.

DBAs Pre-Zuberi

The Courts and Legal Services Act 1990 permits parties to enter into DBAs, and sets out the basic criteria for their validity:

> **58AA Damages-based agreements**
>
> (1) A damages-based agreement which satisfies the conditions in subsection (4) is not unenforceable by reason only of its being a damages-based agreement.
>
> (2) But (subject to subsection (9)) a damages-based agreement which does not satisfy those conditions is unenforceable.
>
> (3) For the purposes of this section—
>
> > (a) a damages-based agreement is an agreement between a person providing advocacy services, litigation services or claims management services and the recipient of those services which provides that—
> >
> > > (i) the recipient is to make a payment to the person providing the services if the recipient obtains a specified financial benefit in connection

with the matter in relation to which the services are provided, and

(ii) the amount of that payment is to be determined by reference to the amount of the financial benefit obtained.

(b) [...]

(4) The agreement—

(a) must be in writing;

(aa) must not relate to proceedings which by virtue of section 58A(1) and (2) cannot be the subject of an enforceable conditional fee agreement or to proceedings of a description prescribed by the Lord Chancellor;

(b) if regulations so provide, must not provide for a payment above a prescribed amount or for a payment above an amount calculated in a prescribed manner;

(c) must comply with such other requirements as to its terms and conditions as are prescribed; and

(d) must be made only after the person providing services under the agreement has complied with such requirements (if any) as may be prescribed as to the provision of information

The Act makes clear that DBAs are unenforceable if they fail to comply with the provisions set out in the Act and relevant regulations, which in this case are the Damages-based Agreements Regulations 2013.

Regulation 1(5) sets out the scope of their application:

... (5) In these Regulations—

(a) regulation 4 does not apply; and

(b) regulations 5, 6, 7 and 8 only apply,

to any damages-based agreement in respect of an employment matter.

The requirements are set out in regulation 3:

3. Requirements of an agreement in respect of all damages-based agreements

The requirements prescribed for the purposes of section 58AA(4)(c) of the Act are that the terms and conditions of a damages-based agreement must specify—

(a) the claim or proceedings or parts of them to which the agreement relates;

(b) the circumstances in which the representative's payment, expenses and costs, or part of them, are payable; and

(c) the reason for setting the amount of the payment at the level agreed, which, in an employment matter, shall include having regard to, where appropriate, whether the claim or proceedings is one of several similar claims or proceedings.

The requirement most relevant for the purposes of the business interruption claims is in regulation 4 (note that 4(2) only applies to personal injury claims):

4. Payment in respect of claims or proceedings other than an employment matter

(1) In respect of any claim or proceedings, other than an employment matter, to which these Regulations apply, a damages-based agreement must not require an amount to be paid by the client other than—

(a) the payment, net of—

(i) any costs (including fixed costs under Part 45 of the Civil Procedure Rules 1998); and

(ii) where relevant, any sum in respect of disbursements incurred by the representative in respect of counsel's fees,

that have been paid or are payable by another party to the proceedings by agreement or order; and

(b) any expenses incurred by the representative, net of any amount which has been paid or is payable by another party to the proceedings by agreement or order.

[(2) In a claim for personal injuries...]

(3) Subject to paragraph (4), in any other claim or proceedings to which this regulation applies, a damages-based agreement must not provide for a payment above an amount which, including VAT, is equal to 50% of the sums ultimately recovered by the client.

The regulation is somewhat confusingly drafted in terms of its practical implications and it has been criticised widely, including by the working group on DBAs and Jackson LJ. Before the *Zuberi* decision, there did not appear to be any plans for reform, and neither was there very much guidance on interpretation of the Regulations in the leading practitioner texts. Before *Zuberi,* no cases had been tested at appellate level and the take-up of DBAs by solicitors has been very low[71]:

71 See Civil Costs, 6th Ed. Chapter 7 at 014.

> **"Problems with damages-based agreements**
>
> Damages-based agreements are not being used. The reason for this is that they are over-regulated and the penalty for failure to comply with the regulations is that the agreement is unenforceable. This is exactly the same situation as arose with the Conditional Fee Agreement Regulations 2000. The first draft of the Damages Based Agreement Regulations was virtually indistinguishable from the earlier CFA Regulations. During the drafting process the senior costs judge urged the drafting team at the Ministry of Justice not to go down the same route and, although some changes were made, the present system is seen as unworkable by the profession."

In October 2014, Jackson LJ said in a speech to the Law Society Conference on "*Commercial Liigation: The Post-Jackson World*":

> "Little use has been made of these provisions. Indeed almost no-one ever enters into a DBA. In particular:
>
> > (i) There is a strong fear that, because of the indemnity principle, the other side will advance technical arguments of the kind that gained popularity (some would say notoriety) during the 'Costs War' over CFAs.
> >
> > (ii) In larger cases solicitors and clients wish to enter 'no win-low fee' DBAs, but there is a fear that these would fall outside the current DBA Regulations.
>
> I do not know who drafted the DBA Regulations and I certainly do not wish to be critical of any particular individuals. The fact remains, however, that the regulations as drafted give rise to a large number of problems. Professor Rachael Mulheron discussed those problems in her article 'The Damages-Based Agreements Regulations 2013: some conundrums in the "Brave New World" of funding'. If the common law 'indemnity principle' is abrogated, as

> recommended in FR [the Review of Civil Litigation Costs Final Report] chapter 5, some of those problems will melt away."

It is important to note a number of features of reg. 4. Sub-paragraph 3 requires that a DBA may not provide for a *payment* (including the VAT) above 50% of the sums recovered by the client. The immediate consequence of that requirement is that if nothing is recovered, nothing can be required to be paid by the client, any payment from the client obviously being higher than half of nothing. That immediately imposes, without being explicit, a "no-win-no-fee" regime, and, indeed, that appears to accord with the intention expressed in the explanatory notes to the regulations.

It is also important to note the slightly less than clear wording of 1(a) and 1(b), both of which use the terminology "net of" when referring to costs, counsel's fees and "expenses" paid or payable by the other side. That is clarified in the explanatory notes to the regulations as follows:

> "Regulation 4, which applies to all DBAs other than those which relate to employment matters, provides that the payment from a client's damages shall be the sum agreed to be paid (which, where relevant, will include any disbursements incurred by the representative in respect of counsel's fees) net of any costs (including fixed costs), or sum in respect of counsel's fees, payable to the representative by another party to the proceedings."

Perhaps leaving some room for misunderstanding, the regulations then provide as follows within their definitions:

> "expenses" means disbursements incurred by the representative, including the expense of obtaining an expert's report and, in an employment matter only, counsel's fees;

> "payment" means that part of the sum recovered in respect of the claim or damages awarded that the client agrees to pay the representative, and excludes expenses but includes,

> in respect of any claim or proceedings to which these regulations apply other than an employment matter, any disbursements incurred by the representative in respect of counsel's fees;
>
> > "representative" means the person providing the advocacy services, litigation services or claims management services to which the damages-based agreement relates.

In an attempt to summarise the pre-*Zuberi* position:

(g) the "payment" (i.e. the success fee element of the DBA) could be no more than 50% of what was recovered;

(h) the "payment" included counsel's fees in BII cases, but in employment cases counsel's fee was an additional expense/disbursement and the effect of this in BII claims was that counsel and solicitors could together charge no more than 50% of the damages including VAT;

(i) the DBA could only provide for payment by the client of "the payment" and, additionally, "expenses", and in any event both have to be reduced by the amount of anything recovered from the other side;

(j) the regulations only applied to first instance proceedings, i.e. appeals could be charged separately;

(k) if a DBA did not conform with those requirements, it was unenforceable under the Act.

Clearly the difficulty with DBAs for solicitors was that they took on all the risk of failure in two circumstances:

(a) where the client proceeds all the way to trial and loses; or

(b) where the client unreasonably withdraws from the litigation after substantial work by the solicitors and counsel.

A reduction of that risk could be achieved by a "hybrid-DBA", i.e. that a lower or discounted fee was charged whatever the outcome, and in the event of a win the DBA percentage could be deducted from damages. Unfortunately, hybrid-DBAs were always thought likely to be in breach of the regulations.

The same risk of unenforceability would probably have arisen where solicitors incorporated terms into the DBA or along-side the DBA which required the client to make payments of solicitors' costs in the event that the client acted unreasonably, although it is fair to say that many DBAs often included similar terms and still do.

In the supplement entitled *Costs & Funding following the Civil Justice Reforms Questions & Answers* 6th Ed. at 2-25 the editors point out that:

> "As noted previously, the indemnity principle has not been disapplied, despite Jackson LJ's recommendation. This is expressly reflected in CPR r.44.18(2)(b) which recites that a party may not recover more by way of costs than the total amount payable under the DBA.
>
> Accordingly, if the "notional/conventional" between the parties costs in a case exceed the sum payable under a DBA, then the between the parties costs recovery will be limited to the DBA sum. However, if the "notional/conventional" between the parties costs are less than the DBA sum, then because the assessment is conducted on that "notional" basis, the between the parties costs recovery will be limited to that conventional sum."

The effect of the indemnity principle not being disapplied leads to the result mentioned in the above extract: that costs could not be recovered from the other side if they amounted to more than the 50% cap under the regulations and that if the DBA was unenforceable for some reason, then the client would not be liable to pay anything to his solicitors, and the other side would therefore not be liable to pay anything to him if he won. Therefore, it is clear that arguments could be made by the other side, in the event of a win, to try and pick apart the DBA to avoid having to pay costs.

Even post-*Zuberi,* despite the obvious attractions of the DBA as a funding model, it will be important to claimants to make sure that the scope for arguing unenforceability is as limited as possible because the other side will have a clear interest in doing so.

Perhaps of some interest, though, is the absence of any requirement in the regulations or commentary that requires the entry into the DBA to be disclosed to the other side, although one could imagine that such disclosure could become contentious during detailed assessment, or even earlier, on an application for security for costs.

DBAs Post-Zuberi

The Zuberi decision was clear in that solicitors are now entitled to charge their time costs in the event that the DBA is terminated by the client. That was a unanimous decision by all three judges and appears to be consistent with how the regulations apply to employment cases, where regulation 8 provides explicitly for termination costs to be chargeable without the DBA becoming unenforceable. The court effectively applied the same principles to non-employment cases even though there is no express provision. The rationale was that the absence of express termination costs in the regulations was a deliberate decision, because solicitors are regulated by the Law Society and SRA and that there was therefore no need to include an express provision regarding termination.

The court, however, went much further. The view of Lewison and Coulson LJJ was that the provisions relating to the percentage could be severed from the rest of the contract of retainer between solicitor and client. Their view was that regulation 4 is only concerned with how the DBA percentage is calculated and does not extend to the entire retainer. Newey LJ dissented.

Newey LJ's dissenting opinion appears to accord entirely with the stated purpose of the regulations, yet the majority view is clear that solicitors are now able to charge not only the DBA percentage, but also time costs on top of that.

Lewison LJ said at para. 38:

> "I can see no objection to regarding that part of the overall agreement relating to recoveries, rather than the whole of the contract of retainer, as amounting to the DBA. In those circumstances, the effect of regulation 4 would control that part of the contract of retainer which dealt with the share of recoveries, but not that part which dealt with time charges."

The consequence of that interpretation is that effective violations of the DBA regulations, which would have rendered the agreement unenforceable but for the *Zuberi* decision, if they appeared elsewhere in the retainer, and did not directly bear on the percentage calculation could still be permissible. That would entitle the solicitors to entirely remove the "no-win-no-fee" character of DBAs by charging their time costs on top of any amounts agreed to be deductible from damages as a percentage. Anticipating the substantial re-characterisation of such agreements, Newey LJ said at paras 64 and 65 (emphasis added):

> "64. The implication, as I understand it, is that neither "sequential hybrid DBAs" nor "concurrent hybrid DBAs" (in the language of the Civil Justice Council's working group) are at present barred. <u>There is nothing to prevent a solicitor agreeing with his client that he will receive up to 50% of the sums ultimately recovered if the claim succeeds and be paid his full time costs if the claim fails. In fact, it would seem to be the case that a retainer could provide for a solicitor to become entitled to both half of recoveries and full time costs in the event of the claim succeeding</u>.
>
> 65. My own view, with respect, is that this construction of the legislation is neither consistent with its history nor borne out by its terms."

Coulson LJ effectively accepted that that was the result of the court's interpretation but took the view it was still permissible for the following reasons (emphasis added):

"82. Thirdly, I am confident that the same result is achieved by consideration of the detail of the Regulations themselves. As I have said, the 'payment' is narrowly defined. Regulation 3 (b) expressly draws a distinction between the payment on the one hand, and the representative's "expenses and costs" on the other. Thus, an entitlement to expenses and costs can, by agreement, be dealt with separately and can be maintained on termination. That is what happened here.

83. Regulation 4(1) is a particular provision designed to incorporate what is known as the Ontario Model. It is solely concerned with the calculation of the final payment, as defined. It has nothing to do with what might be recoverable if the retainer was terminated early. Regulation 4(3) is a cap on the total amount of the payment and again is not concerned with expenses and costs.

84. Thus, the highest that it can be put by the appellant is that Regulation 4(1) could be read as saying that a damages-based agreement must not require any amount to be paid by the client other than the payment itself, and expenses, whatever circumstances may eventuate. So, if the narrow view of a damages-based agreement is not accepted, then, on that literal reading, Regulation 4(1) would, for example, prevent the legal representative from recovering any of its own costs, whatever the retainer actually said, even if the client terminated the agreement without cause after two years of work by the lawyer. That would not only be a commercial nonsense, but it would be contrary to the statutory purpose of section 58AA, which was designed to encourage the use of DBAs, not make them commercial suicide for the lawyer. It would also be contrary to Regulation 3, contrary to the assumptions made about termination provisions to which I have already referred, and render Regulation 8 redundant. I therefore reject that interpretation of Regulation 4(1)."

Unusually, there was a reply to Newey LJ's dissent by Lewison LJ in a post-script at paragraph 50 (emphasis added):

> "**Post-script**
>
> 50. I have, since writing the above, had the benefit of reading the judgment of Newey LJ in draft. I agree with him that the underlying policy was to arrive at the result that he has reached. The difficulty for me is to find that result in the words of the Regulations as drafted. Regulation 4 (1) prohibits the payment of "an amount to be paid by the client other than" those specified in that regulation. The interpretation that Newey LJ prefers is that that prohibition prohibits the payment of "an amount" other than expenses if the claim is lost; but permits payment of "an amount" other than expenses if the retainer is terminated early. Try as I might, I cannot find that reflected in the text of regulation 4. If, however, I am wrong, then I would agree with Newey LJ that, for the reasons he gives, the appeal should be dismissed."

The decision has not been appealed, and the regulations remain as written, opening the door to an array of different types of DBA, previously unavailable.

APPENDIX

SAMPLE PARTICULARS OF CLAIM

IN THE HIGH COURT OF JUSTICE
BUSINESS AND PROPERTY COURTS OF ENGLAND AND WALES
COMMERCIAL COURT (QBD) No. []

BETWEEN:-

Fawcett's Nightclub Ltd.

CLAIMANT

- and -

Wow Insurance Board Plc

DEFENDANT

PARTICULARS OF CLAIM

A. Introduction and Parties

1. The Claimant is a company registered in England and Wales, trading under the names "The Fawcett Club" from premises at 4 Millbank, London (hereinafter "**C**").

2. The Defendant is a public limited company and the insurer in this claim (hereinafter "**D**").

3. D provided C with insurance, including business interruption insurance, under the terms of a policy effective from 2nd August 2019 to 30th March 2020 (hereinafter "**the Policy**").

4. C was closed and suffered losses after the outbreak of COVID-19 in the UK and the imposition of restrictions by the UK Government, and, as particularised below, brings this claim against D for an indemnity under the terms of the Policy.

B. The Policy

5. Attached at **Annex 1** is a copy of the Policy of insurance (No. WOW/Fawc2019/1/2) and Schedule, the content of which C relies on for its full terms and effect as if traversed fully herein.

6. Page 1 of the Schedule confirms that the renewal premium(s) was/were paid by or on behalf of C fully as required by the terms of the Policy, in return for insurance cover in accordance with its terms.

7. Page 4 of the Schedule records, and C avers, the parties' agreement that D would insure C on a "Loss of gross profits" basis (i.e. "Basis 1") up to the overall limit of £15,000,000 over a maximum indemnity period of 12 months arising from interruption to business under the terms of the wording of the Policy. The basis of cover is as set out, inter alia, at page 19 of the Policy, under the heading "*1. Loss of Gross Profits Basis (only operative if indicated in the Schedule)*".

8. Page 7 of the Schedules records, and C avers, the parties' agreement that D would provide an indemnity to C under

clause CPM10: "*CPM10 – Murder, suicide and infectious diseases extension 2006* ("the **Disease Clause**"). That indemnity was agreed to be limited to £100,000, but only for losses arising from avian flu or legionnaires disease, which limit of indemnity, as particularised below, does not apply to this claim.

9. The Disease Clause provided as follows:

CPM10 - Murder, suicide and infectious diseases extension 2006

Section B (Loss of Profits) is extended to include losses arising from the closure of the Premises by a competent authority due to an human notifiable infectious disease or food poisoning suffered by any visitor or employee or by defective sanitation vermin or pests at the Premises as specified in the schedule or by murder or suicide occurring at the Premises.

Notwithstanding the above losses arising from either avian flu or legionnaires diseases are limited to £ 50,000 any one occurrence and in the aggregate

C. Outbreak and Closure of Business

10. The Claimant relies on the factual background relating to the outbreak of COVID-19 in the UK and regulations made, as set out in paragraphs 10 to 52 of the judgment of Flaux LJ and Butcher J in *The Financial Conduct Authority v Arch Insurance (UK) Ltd. and others* [2020] EWHC 2448 (Comm) ("**FCA1**") as if set out herein and in *The Financial Conduct Authority v Arch Insurance (UK) Ltd. and others* [2021] UKSC 1 ("**FCA2**").

<u>Closure of the Premises</u>

11. C closed on **23rd March 2020** and remained closed completely until **4th July 2020** as a result of:

    (a) the following mandatory advice and/or guidance of the UK government:

        i. The guidance given by the Prime Minister, Boris Johnson, in the form of a speech on 16th March 2020, which asked the members of the public to:

"1. self-isolate for 14 days if they or anyone in their household had a high temperature or a new and continuous cough;

2. to stop all non-essential contact with others and to stop all unnecessary travel; to work from home; to avoid pubs, clubs theatres and social venues; and

3. in time, isolate those with serious health conditions from social contact for 12 weeks."

ii. The guidance given by the Prime Minister, Boris Johnson, in the form of a speech on 18th March 2020:

"...So I can announce today and Gavin Williamson making statement now in House of Commons that after schools shut their gates from Friday afternoon, they will remain closed for most pupils – for the vast majority of pupils- until further notice. I will explain what I mean by the vast majority of pupils...."

iii. The guidance given by the Prime Minister, Boris Johnson, in the form of a speech on 20th March 2020:

"...We are collectively telling, telling cafes, pubs, bars, restaurants to close tonight as soon as they reasonably can, and not to open tomorrow. Though to be clear, they can continue to provide take-out services. We're also telling nightclubs, theatres, cinemas, gyms and leisure centres to close on the same timescale...."

(b) restrictions imposed by the "*21 March Regulations*" described in paragraph 34 onwards of FCA1, as amended;

(c) restrictions imposed by the "*26 March Regulations*" described in paragraph 44 onwards of FCA1, as amended;

(d) mandatory advice and/or guidance given on 22nd March 2020, by the Prime Minister who announced the next stage of the UK Government's plan, which included "shielding" measures for vulnerable people and advising members of the public to stay two metres apart even when outdoors;

(e) mandatory advice and/or guidance given on 23rd March 2020, by the Prime Minister saying that it was vital to slow the spread of the disease and "*that's why we have been asking people to stay at home during this pandemic*". He said that the time had come for "*us all to do more*" and said further that he was giving "*the British people a very simple instruction— you must stay at home*". He said that people would only be "*allowed to leave their home*" for very limited purposes such as shopping for basic necessities and "*travelling to and from work, but only where this is absolutely necessary and cannot be done from home*" and "*if you don't follow the rules the police will have the powers to enforce them, including through fines and dispersing gatherings*";

(f) mandatory advice and/or guidance on 23rd March 2020 from Public Health England in a document entitled "*Keeping away from other people: new rules to follow from 23 March 2020*", giving three "*important new rules everyone must follow to stop coronavirus spreading*":

i. "*you must stay at home*" and should only leave home "*if you really need to*" for one of the reasons stated;

ii. most shops should stay closed; and

iii. people must not meet in groups of more than two in public places.

12. C's premises were further closed entirely between January 2021 and March 2021, and subsequently partially closed as a result of restrictions imposed by relevant legislation in operation during

those periods, including the Health Protection (Coronavirus, Restrictions) (No. 3) and (All Tiers) (England) (Amendment) Regulations 2021/8, and C suffered substantial loss during such periods. C avers that such closure, was, likewise, as a result of closure of C's premises by a competent authority due to COVID-19 being suffered by any visitor or employee at C's premises, as well as other cases across the UK. C will rely on specific evidence of manifestation at C's premises during those periods and/or indirect evidence as set out below. In the alternative, the periods of closure in 2021 referred to above were all part of the same public authority intervention which first took place in or around March 2020 as particularised above.

<u>The Disease Clause</u>

13. C avers that the Disease Clause provides cover for "*losses arising from the closure of the Premises by a competent authority due to an human notifiable infectious disease … suffered by any visitor or employee … at the Premises as specified in the schedule…*".

14. C avers that COVID-19 became a notifiable disease on or around 5th March 2020, having been added to Schedule 1 of the Health Protection (Notification) Regulations 2010 (SI 2010/659) ("**the 2010 Regulations**") and further avers that the Disease Clause extends to cover for COVID-19 as "*an human notifiable infectious disease*", the reasonable reader of the provisions of the Disease Clause understanding such wording to refer to those diseases listed under Schedule 1 of the 2010 Regulations.

15. C avers that the facts set out in **Part D. Manifestation** below are sufficient to prove on the balance of probabilities that COVID-19 was suffered by at least one "*visitor or employee … at the Premises as specified in the schedule…*" for the purposes of the Disease Clause and that the term "the Premises" is the address set out at paragraph 1 above, and as a result, cover extends to C.

D. MANIFESTATION

Specific Evidence

16. C avers that COVID-19 was manifested on C's premises and was suffered by at least three employees at C's premises, within the meaning of the Disease Clause prior to the imposition of the restrictions by legislation and/or by guidance referred to above. In particular,

    (a) on or around 6th March 2020, C's employee Joseph Bloggs suffered from COVID-19 and was hospitalised on 10th March 2020 due to COVID-19; and

    (b) C's employee Justine Smith, suffered from COVID-19 on or around 15th March 2020, was subsequently hospitalised and died due to COVID-19 on 18th April 2020;

    (c) C's employee Kylie Kay, suffered from COVID-19 on or around 5th March 2020, was subsequently hospitalised and died due to COVID-19 on 2nd April 2020;

Indirect Evidence

17. C will further rely on the following facts to show that it was more likely than not that at least one "*visitor or employee … at the Premises*" suffered from COVID-19 prior to the closure of the premises described above:

    (a) the square footage of the premises is around 15,000 sqft, being sufficiently large an area and, as set out below, having on it a significant number of people during opening times;

    (b) the premises was normally open in the evenings between, Thursday to Saturday each week;

(c) the number of people usually present on the premises varied, but usually comprised about 800 customers and 60 staff;

(d) NHS deaths data for the area(s) in which C's premises are situated;

(e) ONS deaths data for the area(s) in which C's premises are situated;

(f) UK government reported cases of COVID-19 for the area(s) in which C's premises are situated;

(g) the presence of sites of concentrated infections such as hospitals, care homes, clinics or other such sites in proximity to C's premises;

(h) C's premises is within the Millbank area of London and the FCA COVID Calculator shows estimated cases as at this address and within one mile thereof as at 23rd March 2020. It shows as at that date that there were 100 cumulative cases. Imperial College Data is made available on the FCA Website[72]. It shows that there were 110 new estimated cases and 1,500 cumulative cases estimated for that date for the area at and within a mile of the Premises. The figures also demonstrate that COVID-19 was likely occurring at C's premises as being within the area throughout the period of indemnity. A copy of the report is attached at **Annex 4**.

18. C therefore avers that at least one "*visitor or employee … at the Premises*" suffered from COVID-19.

72https://www.fca.org.uk/publications/finalised-guidance/business-interruption-insurance-test-case-proving-presence-coronavirus

19. C will further rely on statistical/actuarial expert evidence, informed in part by the facts set out above, to prove such manifestation of COVID-19 at C's premises.

E. CAUSATION

20. C relies upon the test of causation set out in **FCA2**, set out at paragraph 212 (emphasis added):

> "212. We conclude that, on the proper interpretation of the disease clauses, <u>in order to show that loss from interruption of the insured business was proximately caused by one or more occurrences of illness resulting from COVID-19, it is sufficient to prove that the interruption was a result of Government action taken in response to cases of disease which included at least one case of COVID-19 within the geographical area covered by the clause</u>. The basis for this conclusion is the analysis of the court below, which in our opinion is correct, that each of the individual cases of illness resulting from COVID-19 which had occurred by the date of any Government action was a separate and equally effective cause of that action (and of the response of the public to it). Our conclusion does not depend on the particular terminology used in the clause to describe the required causal connection between the loss and the insured peril and applies equally whether the term used is "following" or some other formula such as "arising from" or "as a result of". It is a conclusion about the legal effect of the insurance contracts as they apply to the facts of this case."

21. C avers that the restrictions set out in **Part C.** above amounted to closure by a competent authority.

22. C further avers that the advice/guidance referred to in **Part C.** above was in such mandatory terms so as to have reasonably amounted to closure by a competent authority.

23. Due to at least one "*visitor or employee ... at the Premises*" suffering from COVID-19, as pleaded in **Part D.** above, along with other cases of COVID-19 (per paragraph 212 of FCA2) C avers that the UK Government issued the advice/guidance and/or enacted legislation as set out in **Part C.** above, which amounted to closure of the C's premises, causing loss to C.

24. C therefore avers that the facts as set out above trigger cover under the Disease Clause such that C is entitled to an indemnity from D under the terms of the Policy in the sum set out in **Part F.** below and that on a true construction of the policy there is no difference or distinction to be drawn between clauses which specify the relevant policy area by reference to a radius, such as "1 mile", and the wording above defining the relevant policy area as "the premises". C avers that the commercial purpose of the clause would be defeated were such a distinction to be drawn, especially given its reference to notifiable diseases (an open-ended list of diseases, which by their nature could, spread rapidly and widely). C therefore avers that the public authority restrictions were "*due to*" the developing and aggregate prevalence of COVID-19 across the UK including at the Premises.

F. Resulting Loss

25. C's management accounts for 2020/2021 are attached hereto at **Annex 2** and C relies on them to demonstrate its loss. Was closed or substantially closed between March 2020 and March 2021, divided into sixteen 4-week (sometimes 5-week) periods as shown in the management accounts. The gross profit for the preceding year per relevant period was £[]. The gross profit received during the period of closure was approximately £[].

26. **Annex 3** demonstrates C's total loss of gross profits due under Basis 1 based on the operation of the Disease Clause is currently estimated to be £[] and with adjustments based on the trends clauses at page 18 of the Policy wording, and detailed at **Annex** 3, the figure claimed by C is **£10,000,000.**

27. C claims interest on the said sum at the annual rate of 4% from 23rd March 2020 until the date of judgment pursuant to s.35A of The Senior Courts Act 1981.

28. C therefore claims the said sum along with interest as a contractual indemnity from D.

29. C further avers that D has wrongfully, unreasonably and in breach of its obligations under the Policy, failed to indemnify C under the above terms of the Policy by paying the said sums due in respect of its losses.

30. Further, C has suffered loss and damage by reason of D's breach of its obligations in such similar sum as aforesaid, in particular for failing to pay sums due in respect of the claim within a reasonable time, and is entitled to a declaration to that effect and damages with interest thereon under s.13A of the Insurance Act 2015.

AND THE CLAIMANT CLAIMS:-

(a) Indemnity and damages;

(b) Interest thereon, as set out above;

(c) The declaration claimed in paragraph 30 above;

(d) Costs;

(e) Further or other relief.

1st September 2021

NEIL FAWCETT

Statement of Truth

*(I believe)(The Claimant believes) that the facts stated in these particulars of claim are true.

I understand that proceedings for contempt of court may be brought against anyone who makes, or causes to be made, a false statement in a document verified by a statement of truth without an honest belief in its truth.

*I am duly authorised by the claimant to sign this statement

Full name ....

Name of Claimant's solicitor's firm ....

Signed .... position or office held ....

*[Claimant] [Litigation friend] [Claimant's solicitor] (if signing on behalf of firm or company)

*delete as appropriate

[Name and address of claimant or claimant's solicitors]

MORE BOOKS BY LAW BRIEF PUBLISHING

A selection of our other titles available now:-

'A Practical Guide to Transgender Law' by Robin Moira White & Nicola Newbegin
'Artificial Intelligence – The Practical Legal Issues (2nd Edition)' by John Buyers
'A Practical Guide to Challenging Sham Marriage Allegations in Immigration Law' by Priya Solanki
'A Practical Guide to New Build Conveyancing' by Paul Sams & Rebecca East
'A Practical Guide to Inherited Wealth on Divorce' by Hayley Trim
'A Practical Guide to Shareholder Disputes in Family Businesses' by Ed Weeks
'A Practical Guide to the Law of Forests in Scotland' by Philip Buchan
'A Practical Guide to Health and Medical Cases in Immigration Law' by Rebecca Chapman & Miranda Butler
'A Practical Guide to Bad Character Evidence for Criminal Practitioners by Aparna Rao
'A Practical Guide to Environmental Enforcement' by Christopher Badger & Stuart Jessop
'A Practical Guide to Hoarding and Mental Health for Housing Lawyers' by Rachel Coyle
'A Practical Guide to Psychiatric Claims in Personal Injury – 2nd Edition' by Liam Ryan
'Stephens on Contractual Indemnities' by Richard Stephens
'A Practical Guide to the EU Succession Regulation' by Richard Frimston
'A Practical Guide to Solicitor and Client Costs – 2nd Edition' by Robin Dunne
'Constructive Dismissal – Practice Pointers and Principles' by Benjimin Burgher
'A Practical Guide to Religion and Belief Discrimination Claims in the Workplace' by Kashif Ali
'A Practical Guide to the Law of Medical Treatment Decisions' by Ben Troke

'Fundamental Dishonesty and QOCS in Personal Injury Proceedings: Law and Practice' by Jake Rowley
'A Practical Guide to the Law in Relation to School Exclusions' by Charlotte Hadfield & Alice de Coverley
'A Practical Guide to Divorce for the Silver Separators' by Karin Walker
'The Right to be Forgotten – The Law and Practical Issues' by Melissa Stock
'A Practical Guide to Planning Law and Rights of Way in National Parks, the Broads and AONBs' by James Maurici QC, James Neill et al
'A Practical Guide to Election Law' by Tom Tabori
'A Practical Guide to the Law in Relation to Surrogacy' by Andrew Powell
'A Practical Guide to Claims Arising from Fatal Accidents – 2nd Edition' by James Patience
'A Practical Guide to the Ownership of Employee Inventions – From Entitlement to Compensation' by James Tumbridge & Ashley Roughton
'A Practical Guide to Asbestos Claims' by Jonathan Owen & Gareth McAloon
'A Practical Guide to Stamp Duty Land Tax in England and Northern Ireland' by Suzanne O'Hara
'A Practical Guide to the Law of Farming Partnerships' by Philip Whitcomb
'Covid-19, Homeworking and the Law – The Essential Guide to Employment and GDPR Issues' by Forbes Solicitors
'Covid-19, Force Majeure and Frustration of Contracts – The Essential Guide' by Keith Markham
'Covid-19 and Criminal Law – The Essential Guide' by Ramya Nagesh
'Covid-19 and Family Law in England and Wales – The Essential Guide' by Safda Mahmood
'A Practical Guide to the Law of Unlawful Eviction and Harassment – 2nd Edition' by Stephanie Lovegrove
'Covid-19, Residential Property, Equity Release and Enfranchisement – The Essential Guide' by Paul Sams and Louise Uphill
'Covid-19, Brexit and the Law of Commercial Leases – The Essential Guide' by Mark Shelton
'A Practical Guide to Costs in Personal Injury Claims – 2nd Edition' by Matthew Hoe

'A Practical Guide to the General Data Protection Regulation (GDPR) – 2nd Edition' by Keith Markham

'Ellis on Credit Hire – Sixth Edition' by Aidan Ellis & Tim Kevan

'A Practical Guide to Working with Litigants in Person and McKenzie Friends in Family Cases' by Stuart Barlow

'Protecting Unregistered Brands: A Practical Guide to the Law of Passing Off' by Lorna Brazell

'A Practical Guide to Secondary Liability and Joint Enterprise Post-Jogee' by Joanne Cecil & James Mehigan

'A Practical Guide to the Pre-Action RTA Claims Protocol for Personal Injury Lawyers' by Antonia Ford

'A Practical Guide to Neighbour Disputes and the Law' by Alexander Walsh

'A Practical Guide to Forfeiture of Leases' by Mark Shelton

'A Practical Guide to Coercive Control for Legal Practitioners and Victims' by Rachel Horman

'A Practical Guide to Rights Over Airspace and Subsoil' by Daniel Gatty

'Tackling Disclosure in the Criminal Courts – A Practitioner's Guide' by Narita Bahra QC & Don Ramble

'A Practical Guide to the Law of Driverless Cars – Second Edition' by Alex Glassbrook, Emma Northey & Scarlett Milligan

'A Practical Guide to TOLATA Claims' by Greg Williams

'A Practical Guide to Elderly Law – 2nd Edition' by Justin Patten

'A Practical Guide to the Law of Prescription in Scotland' by Andrew Foyle

'A Practical Guide to the Construction and Rectification of Wills and Trust Instruments' by Edward Hewitt

'A Practical Guide to the Law of Bullying and Harassment in the Workplace' by Philip Hyland

'How to Be a Freelance Solicitor: A Practical Guide to the SRA-Regulated Freelance Solicitor Model' by Paul Bennett

'A Practical Guide to Prison Injury Claims' by Malcolm Johnson

'A Practical Guide to the Small Claims Track - 2nd Edition' by Dominic Bright

'A Practical Guide to Advising Clients at the Police Station' by Colin Stephen McKeown-Beaumont

'A Practical Guide to Antisocial Behaviour Injunctions' by Iain Wightwick
'Practical Mediation: A Guide for Mediators, Advocates, Advisers, Lawyers, and Students in Civil, Commercial, Business, Property, Workplace, and Employment Cases' by Jonathan Dingle with John Sephton
'The Mini-Pupillage Workbook' by David Boyle
'A Practical Guide to Crofting Law' by Brian Inkster
'A Practical Guide to Spousal Maintenance' by Liz Cowell
'A Practical Guide to the Law of Domain Names and Cybersquatting' by Andrew Clemson
'A Practical Guide to the Law of Gender Pay Gap Reporting' by Harini Iyengar
'A Practical Guide to the Rights of Grandparents in Children Proceedings' by Stuart Barlow
'NHS Whistleblowing and the Law' by Joseph England
'Employment Law and the Gig Economy' by Nigel Mackay & Annie Powell
'A Practical Guide to Noise Induced Hearing Loss (NIHL) Claims' by Andrew Mckie, Ian Skeate, Gareth McAloon
'An Introduction to Beauty Negligence Claims – A Practical Guide for the Personal Injury Practitioner' by Greg Almond
'Intercompany Agreements for Transfer Pricing Compliance' by Paul Sutton
'Zen and the Art of Mediation' by Martin Plowman
'A Practical Guide to the SRA Principles, Individual and Law Firm Codes of Conduct 2019 – What Every Law Firm Needs to Know' by Paul Bennett
'A Practical Guide to Adoption for Family Lawyers' by Graham Pegg
'A Practical Guide to Industrial Disease Claims' by Andrew Mckie & Ian Skeate
'A Practical Guide to Redundancy' by Philip Hyland
'A Practical Guide to Vicarious Liability' by Mariel Irvine
'A Practical Guide to Applications for Landlord's Consent and Variation of Leases' by Mark Shelton
'A Practical Guide to Relief from Sanctions Post-Mitchell and Denton' by Peter Causton
'A Practical Guide to Equity Release for Advisors' by Paul Sams
'A Practical Guide to Financial Services Claims' by Chris Hegarty

'The Law of Houses in Multiple Occupation: A Practical Guide to HMO Proceedings' by Julian Hunt

'Occupiers, Highways and Defective Premises Claims: A Practical Guide Post-Jackson – 2nd Edition' by Andrew Mckie

'A Practical Guide to Financial Ombudsman Service Claims' by Adam Temple & Robert Scrivenor

'A Practical Guide to Advising Schools on Employment Law' by Jonathan Holden

'A Practical Guide to Running Housing Disrepair and Cavity Wall Claims: 2nd Edition' by Andrew Mckie & Ian Skeate

'A Practical Guide to Holiday Sickness Claims – 2nd Edition' by Andrew Mckie & Ian Skeate

'Arguments and Tactics for Personal Injury and Clinical Negligence Claims' by Dorian Williams

'A Practical Guide to Drone Law' by Rufus Ballaster, Andrew Firman, Eleanor Clot

'A Practical Guide to Compliance for Personal Injury Firms Working With Claims Management Companies' by Paul Bennett

'RTA Allegations of Fraud in a Post-Jackson Era: The Handbook – 2nd Edition' by Andrew Mckie

'RTA Personal Injury Claims: A Practical Guide Post-Jackson' by Andrew Mckie

'On Experts: CPR35 for Lawyers and Experts' by David Boyle

'An Introduction to Personal Injury Law' by David Boyle

'A Practical Guide to Subtle Brain Injury Claims' by Pankaj Madan

These books and more are available to order online direct from the publisher at www.lawbriefpublishing.com, where you can also read free sample chapters. For any queries, contact us on 0844 587 2383 or mail@lawbriefpublishing.com.

Our books are also usually in stock at www.amazon.co.uk with free next day delivery for Prime members, and at good legal bookshops such as Wildy & Sons.

We are regularly launching new books in our series of practical day-to-day practitioners' guides. Visit our website and join our free newsletter to be kept informed and to receive special offers, free chapters, etc.

You can also follow us on Twitter at www.twitter.com/lawbriefpub.

www.ingramcontent.com/pod-product-compliance
Lightning Source LLC
LaVergne TN
LVHW022041200926
848481LV00003B/741